Focus Puller

Daniel Hess

Table of Contents

Lily 1

Magnolia 3

Kill Your Darlings 7

Sometimes They Come Back Again 15

Under the Skin 20

Lily II 26

Drive 28

Only Lovers Left Alive 34

The Hunt 40

Prisoners 44

Julia 47

Arrival 51

Fool's Gold 55

As Above, So Below 60

The Invisible Guest 65

Gravity 72

Lily III 75

Warm Bodies 78

The Call 85

The Company You Keep 91

Dunkirk 100

Parasite 106

Heather 120

Ex Machina 123

Bethany 130

Climax 136

The Neon Demon 141

Paprika 150

Missy 160

What Dreams May Come 163

Perfect Blue 167

Jackie 174

The Circle 177

Knock Knock 184

Mary 196

Us 199

Blue Valentine 206

Dogtooth 214

Megan 220

Gone Girl 224

The Glass House 231

Children of Men 235

Lamb 242

Fargo 247

Afterword

Copyright © 2022 Tony Productions All rights reserved.

No part of this book may be reproduced, or stored in a retrieval system, or transmitted in any form or by any means, electronic, mechanical, photocopying, recording, or otherwise, without express written permission of the publisher.

Cover Design Credit: Sandra Boskamp:

Sandra Boskamp is an artist based in the United States whose paintings have been exhibited nationally. She describes her pieces as fusing fluid and organic line work with contemporary photography that draws inspiration from technology contrasted with tradition. Through her art, Boskamp hopes to evoke "the feeling of something fading away from past norms". She primarily creates using oils and enamel on canvas.

Lily

Ben…a name I wish I could forget, but one that haunts me constantly. Well, I guess if I'm going to talk about it, I might as well start at the beginning.

We met on Myspace, way back when that was still a thing. I remember they introduced these little group boards where you could join in depending on what year you were graduating high school. Not every grade had one and they had to be started by an admin. I was in the one for class of 2010, but I happened upon the class of 2008.

There, I stumbled upon Benjamin; I don't even recall what particularly stood out about him. Maybe it was the profile song, or maybe just his blue eyes. Whatever it was, I sent him a message that day, sitting at the shared computer in my grandparents' house in the basement. It was probably in-between sessions of playing The Sims back then.

After a few times of messaging numbers were exchanged. Then it became texting and we decided to meet after school one day.

It was spring and Ben promised to show me what everyone used to call Marioland in the woods behind the school. There were a bunch of old pipes, all abandoned or something. I never would see it, but the trail that led to it hosted many smokers, stoners and just people skipping class.

We walked and walked with Ben leading the way. He kept saying he could find it, but we never did. Instead, he awkwardly suggested heading up a small hill that was clear of branches or trees. Back then we did the natural early teenage thing and began kissing, then making out.

It wasn't my first time kissing a boy but it was my first time feeling so passionate with one. He tried pulling up my shirt a few times and although I didn't say anything directly it made me feel really uncomfortable. I think he got the message though as he stopped after a few times.

We left the woods and I think his dad came to pick him up. My grandmother got me and neither one of us acknowledged the other's parental figures. We texted for a little while and I thought it would be funny to mention I got my period right after he left. He must have not found it funny, as he stopped messaging me and we didn't talk again for almost two years.

Magnolia

That green box, that translucent green box was the start of so many possibilities. Each cartridge that would ever be shoved into its various pin connectors would unlock a world unlike the last. Adventures awaited, frustration lurked and, most importantly of all, memories were to be made.

This was a weekend of sleepover fun for Ben and his cousin Anthony, a time to forget about all the troubles of the world and just enjoy the escape. What was on tap for this evening? A helping of Mario Kart 64 followed by South Park: The Game. The latter of which was Anthony's chance to completely decimate Ben in multiplayer shenanigans. The phrase "I fart on your grave" would echo for decades to come as so often remembered by Anthony's mother.

No matter what, though, Ben could never stay mad at Anthony or as he would call him, Tony for short.

After the videogames were played until they both got tired of them, it was time to watch whatever was on cable tv that night. Saturday evenings were kind of a crap shoot in that nothing new was really premiering, so it was a lot of reruns to sift through. Wrestling was always on Mondays and Wednesdays, which would have been the next logical choice in programming to bond over.

Where things landed was Cartoon Network with repeats of old episodes of *Dexter's Lab* and *Powerpuff Girls*. The channel would change, though, when the girls filled the screen. The two boys quickly would head to MTV where *Jackass* was playing that night.

As it grew later in the evening all the shows that Ben's father explicitly forbid would become quick viewing for them both.

In fact, this place represented all the things that Ben was deprived of at home. The freedom to watch whatever he wanted, candy in open jars and no parental controls to speak of. It was a true mecca, away from the more oppressive style that his parents kept tightly locked down. Even swearing was a no-go at home, whereas here the slang words Ben had never even heard before were uttered with little thought given. It was a wildly unique experience.

This wanting to be adjacent to off the wall situations is something that would turn into a desire for Ben in later years of life, but for now it was simply a passing fascination.

As the night started to wind down into the dreaded fighting to keep the eyes open, the two boys decided it was time for bed. Ben was trying to fight for the party to keep going, but Tony was simply too tired.

When they made the way over to the bedroom Tony climbed up to the top bunk of his bunkbed, which he shared with his younger brother Brian. Brian was away that weekend, so Ben took the bottom bunk and felt like he was taking the true brotherly place he always wanted to occupy.

In the final moments before passing out, Ben had so many questions he still wanted to ask, but he landed on one in particular.

"Where do dreams come from?"

"My teacher told us they are like these sparks of light that fire in your brain. When they go off faster and faster you have a dream."

"So, it is like light hitting your eyes?"

"The most amazing light you've ever seen buddy. If you remember your dreams tonight tell me about them tomorrow, okay?"

"Okay."

A few more deep breaths and Ben fell asleep soundly. The dreams came flooding in, but by the morning sun they were all gone, left in the ether of time.

Kill Your Darlings

He was warm, he was happy, he was content. All the things he had every wanted to see he saw, and all the goals he wished to accomplish were finished. And then he woke up.

Ben started his day buried under a cocoon of blankets laying close to his girlfriend of five years, Lily. It was early in the morning, still dark outside, and he awoke to a home of responsibility. As soon as she saw the first rumblings from under the blanket his dog, Roxy, jumped out from her crate as she knew she would soon be fed.

Ben and Lily slept on the floor that evening, not out of some sort of fun escape from the monotony of the same bed, but rather due to the fact that the second level of their townhome was so frigid. It was the end of fall and the beginning of winter in Maryland, and upstairs in this rented home one of the windows would not fully shut. Ben had called management about the window and they sent their underpaid, overaged repair man to take a look. He finagled the window shut but during the warmer months, a slight nudge to crack the window bolted it right back into its now rigid state.

With his limited knowledge of handy homework, Ben did the best he could with duct tape, but the draft remained. So, they kept the door to the room shut, slowing the cold breeze as much as they could. This fix served double duty for the young couple, as this also kept Roxy and their two pet cats, Juno and Hiss, separated. Roxy did not get along with other dogs too well so they had a fear that she might be violent toward Juno and Hiss.

As Ben rose and Roxy rushed over, Lily stayed asleep under the covers. She would more than likely not rise for the next three or four hours, Ben thought. Ben felt that cold air rushing toward him like a hungry linebacker chasing after a cornerback. The first thing he had to do was pee, which involved going up the stairs to the bathroom. Each step up felt like a ten degree drop in temperature, but it was the only bathroom in the house. Roxy bumbled behind Ben up the steps, - she loved to sniff the door where the cats stayed as they stuck their paws scratching at the air through the gap.

Ben put out the food for Roxy and let her out. He loved looking out the door, watching Roxy burst through in the morning into the big open courtyard behind the home. Even though it was a shared space, this early in the morning no one was out, so Roxy had free rein to explore. Ben always bore a smile on his face when he saw Roxy running about, rolling in the grass. It was like for another moment he was free, running through nature with a childlike sense of discovery. Today though, with the cold breeze, he did not want to disturb Lily, so he shut the door and got to preparing the food for Juno and Hiss.

Juno was named after the film character whose indie drama Ben and Lily bonded over early in their dating life. Hiss was named so for her short fuse. The two were sisters, nearly identical outside of their temperament. As Ben went back up the steps, he knew that the moment he opened the door to the room they would both try and jump past the door and into the rest of the home. It was pretty obvious from the way in which they completely shredded the carpet trying to dig themselves out from this confinement. It was cruel and Ben always felt bad, but Lily had the cats long before they moved into the townhome and with no one else to foster them, this was the only answer for the time being.

After stopping their escape, Ben put down the food and the cats were for a moment at least lulled into a state of content for their tiny surroundings. Before leaving the room, Ben saw a hairball on the sheets of the bed where he and Lily used to reside, - he would deal with it later.

Now after about thirty minutes of initial morning chores, Ben was finally able to sit down to his own breakfast. As he opened the fridge, he could tell that cold air was not reaching it the way it should. Another quirk of this townhouse was the freezer, which would often freeze over, making the fridge warm if not kept in check. When this happened, Ben would have to take everything out of the fridge and freezer, place it in a cooler and use Lily's hairdryer to thaw out the block of ice which was preventing the cold air from billowing down into the fridge compartments below.

If Ben was lucky, this would happen once every two weeks and would take up about an hour of his day. Today was not a lucky day, and Ben knew that another chore would be to thaw the freezer out again. The milk smelled as if it was turning, but Ben pushed on anyway with his routine of mixing, raisin bran and flavored cheerios (today it was pumpkin spice) in a bowl with milk. On the side Ben would prepare a piece of toast with butter and plenty of garlic.

Roxy finished her breakfast before Ben and returned to her crate, a now satisfied pup. Ben gave her a nice pat on the head and returned to finishing his food in the quiet kitchen. His toast was quickly getting cold, so he scarfed everything down and put the dirty plates in the sink. Whether driven by boredom or routine, Ben immediately did the dishes and sat them in the tray next to the sink to dry.

He turned out the kitchen light and looked out into the living room, which was slowly gaining light with the first of the morning sun. It was going to be a bright day despite the cold, and Ben looked over, seeing Lily still sleeping peacefully. He wished he could still be lying next to her, but his need to get his day started early outweighed the wants of his affection. It would be a barrier he would struggle with for years to come.

He again walked upstairs, facing the cold to get to his computer. It sat against a white wall, not uncommon in this home as the walls were all white, in a hand me down, beat up desk that Ben had acquired from his parents. In lieu of a proper chair to sit in, Ben had a storage box that he used as his seat for working from the computer. The room was stacked with storage boxes that were never properly unpacked from the initial move into this home, and would never be until they, moved out in only 9 more months when the lease was set to expire.

Ben took his usual time looking through the morning Craigslist ads trying to find extra gigs to make money outside of the two part time jobs he was already working. Ben had graduated from college only a year prior with a Bachelor's of Science degree in Electronic Media and Film from Towson

University. It was something he earned, but also something that did not make much actual difference in the world Ben found himself in. Every job, gig, or short-term assignment Ben would ever take on never took this degree into account.

On this day Ben found a few leads to look over and responded to them thusly:

"To whom it may concern,

My name is Ben Williams and I was reaching out today concerning your ad on Craigslist looking for a videographer. I have attached a few links to my previous work below. I currently film with a Canon 5D Mark III and a Canon 6D as my second camera when needed. I have a full slate of audio as well as LED lighting gear and travel is no problem for me.

Website link.

Thank you very much for your time and consideration,

Ben Williams"

This was so deeply ingrained in Ben's mind that he could practically write it in his sleep. However, besides his two normal jobs, this gave Ben a sense of control over his life and what he could accomplish. Each small gig he could book outside of work was extra money that would go toward rent, the pets, and any other emergencies that could pop up, which seemed to be far too many at this point in life.

Ben shut down his computer and went over to the bathroom, where he would face the thing that really made or broke the rest of his day for him. Ben was an anxious young man and for Ben, his morning bowel movement carried a lot of weight. Some days it came easy, some days it could take up to an hour. Either way, Ben developed his own system of helping things along the way. After about fifteen minutes of watching videos on his phone, Ben would take a bottle of conditioner which he kept under the sink and lube his pinky up. After this lubrication, Ben would take his pinky and put it up his rectum, to lubricate and stimulate his movement along. There was no pleasurable sensation in the act for Ben, but one of necessity to help things along.

Even still, this process could take an hour to accomplish, so he knew by the time he was done Lily would just be waking up. It was an easy way to avoid any questions by Lily as to what would take so long and also hide the shame of hogging the bathroom from her in the morning. Today was to be a productive day, as Ben had a nice healthy bowel movement which left him feeling "cleaned out," it was a certain feeling that

Ben could sense in his stomach that just seemed right and that sensation hit nicely on this morning.

As Ben was walking back down the steps, he hoped that Lily was still asleep, for if she was, he knew he could lay down next to her for at least a little bit longer. He saw she still was, so he quietly went back under the covers, gave her a kiss on the cheek, and pulled her close. As he did, he laid his phone off to the side. With it now on silent, he did not receive the notification from his email account.

That email, although not known at the time by Ben, Lily, or anyone close to them, would change the way Ben would go through the world for the rest of Ben's life.

Sometimes They Come Back Again

Ben's father laid on the asphalt as he worked on his current pride and joy, a 1995 Jaguar XJS which ran like a dream when it wanted to run. The routine was to stay out of the light and hand the tools over when needed.

Eventually, frustration would set in and the uncomfortable moments of his father getting irate with a part of the vehicle not functioning correctly or just being hard to reach. What started as a joke about the poor engineering or design would quickly devolve into grunting or raised voices. When things would get too loud, Ben's mother would come outside to bring Ben back into the house.

An apology was given after the fact, always after the fact. It was never stated before then. Something that Ben would echo in his worst moments between his later teenage years and early twenties.

The boundaries were always set with the gender lines in this household, too. Ben's mother would rarely be involved with anything involving car repair. Her excuses would always be boredom or just the self-defeating attitude of not understanding any of it, even though she could have learned at any point through practice.

This disjointed nature would be an ever-growing trend that Ben didn't even realize until he was much older. His mother had her projects and his father had his. It was beneficial in that it opened the door to different types of projects and differing perspectives from both of his parents.

After a little while of working, Ben's father invited him to come under the car.

"Do you wanna see it?"

"Can I?!"

"Don't tell your mother."

Ben quickly got on his back and scooted under the vehicle where he was treated to a plethora of parts that he didn't understand the first thing about. The metals bits were bent all about, creating this uniform yet disjointed balance of dirty, functioning goodness.

In his excitement, he began reaching upwards to touch everything, not even realizing how quickly his hands were being blackened from all the soot and debris caked on to the various pieces.

His father was trying to point things out to Ben as if to try to get the bits from blurred mess to some bit of cohesion. It was in one ear and out the other, but it was fun for the short time it lasted all the same.

Without notice, the soot started to sprinkle down and happened to fall into Ben's eyes. For a second it seemed fine, nothing was wrong but Ben's father knew what had just happened. Tears began to form and the crying started.

Rather than remaining calm about the situation, it all ramped up to a bunch of shouting for Ben's mother to rush out and help. Had it just been a calm exchange and a walk inside the home to get the eyes rinsed out, it might not have been anything major but the crying only grew louder as Ben's mother rushed out, almost yelling about what was going on.

As his father explained, Ben was stuck blinded by the dirt and tears. He was picked up and carried into the home. His mother irate with his father over allowing him to sit under the car, while saying some tender words that proved rather ineffective in the heat of everything else.

After some water splashing and paper towel dabbing, his the eyes were cleared off and Ben was plopped down on the living room couch. His mother turned on some cartoons and gave him a small bag of Pizzeria Chips.

Feeling content with the status of her son she moved over to talk to Ben's father.

"Why did you let him under the car?"

"I was trying to show the boy how it all worked. He was interested in it and I guess his excitement got the better of me. What do you want me to say?"

"You should know better than that. He could have gone blind."

"I know, I know. I should have given him some safety glasses to wear."

"Just don't do it again."

His parents thought that Ben couldn't hear over the droning TV, but he made sure to focus his attention on the conversation. The arguing persisted and Ben watched his father go outside to lower the Jaguar back down.

The next day Ben wanted to try again to lay under the car to take a look, but his father wouldn't allow it this time.

"Next time, Benjamin."

Rather than a next time, working on the vehicle as the ever-trusted hander of tools would become the official emblem that Ben would wear for a few more years to come. His interest in the vehicle work would dissipate as the years grew on. Perhaps it was for the best, but who knows what would have happened if that day went differently.

Under the Skin

It was about forty-five minutes later when Lily finally woke up. She was a heavy sleeper and did not hear Ben get up for his morning routine. As she slowly started to come to, she greeted Ben, who was still asleep a poke on the side of his stomach. After a few jabs Ben was awake.

"Good morning," Ben said yawning.

"Morning," Lily said as she let out a big stretch.

"Do you want any breakfast?"

"Did you eat already?"

"Yes," Ben said softly.

"You never wait for me."

"Sorry, I just wake up and I'm hungry, we'll have breakfast together soon I promise." In fact, for the entirety of the stay at this rented home Ben and Lily would never have a single breakfast in unison.

"How about I make you something." Ben got up after giving Lily a few kisses and walked toward the kitchen, as Roxy followed behind. Ben looked around the now even warmer fridge which held scarce traces of food. He thought he could make eggs, but they didn't have any. Perhaps a pancake but he didn't even know where to start with those, no waffles, no bacon, with Lily working late night shifts it was clear that any sort of breakfast food was clearly lacking. In fact, this was the first time in a long while that Lily was up before 11a.m.

Lily slowly made her way into the kitchen, still stretching and yawning. Her oversized shirt barely covered over her panties. Ben always admired her cute bubbly demeanor, made all the more evident in the morning haze that Lily was still coming out from. She had porcelain pale skin, complete with a few piercings to give her that edgy style Ben always fantasized he'd have in a girlfriend growing up watching too many music videos on MTV. Lily was pleasantly plump in her body size, not too skinny, but not overweight by any stretch of the imagination. It was perfect for Ben, who himself was a bit on the scrawny side, having lost weight since he began counting his calories each day.

There she sat, petting Roxy and waiting for what Ben might conjure up. She had hardly a clue of what actually was in the house, working as a server meant that many of her meals were end of shift dinners prepared as they closed the kitchen or next day leftovers that she grabbed up before leaving which would be thrown away that night anyway. This was all foreign to her and she was expecting a good guide out of Ben.

Out of fresh ideas, and notably food, Ben put together some cereal in a bowl and made toast. It was his only option but luckily for him Lily's appetite outweighed any need for something fancy. She was delighted to eat the cereal and it reminded her of early mornings before school at her grandparents' home where she spent most of her adolescence. It was a safe nostalgia trip and while they weren't eating together it was nice that they could share this time in the morning usually reserved for sleeping and Ben's necessity for routine.

After eating, Lily took a pit stop in the bedroom to play with the cats for a little bit. In this in-between, Ben stayed downstairs to fold up the blankets from their makeshift bed. He enjoyed another task to accomplish and got the living room straightened up as if no blanket bed had ever existed. He realized though that today, after Lily left for work it would be another salting day. About once a week, Ben would buy a large container of salt to lay in the carpet to fight the flea infestation they had been dealing with since first moving in. They could not stay in a hotel since Roxy was such a large dog and did not want to risk staying with family and leaving them with fleas in order to have an exterminator fumigate. After Google research Ben discovered that salt would dry out and kill fleas along with their eggs, a tactic which seemed to be working in conjunction with heavy bathing for all the animals in flea shampoo.

Lily finished up with the cats and went to the bathroom. Ben finally had a chance to look through his phone to check on any emails. He had one new one from a name he had never seen before, it was addressed from Jeff Williams and was a response to an ad of his own he had placed on Craigslist advertising Wedding Video Services. The email read:

"To whom it may concern,

My name is Jeff Williams and I represent Williams Photography. I'm local here in the Baltimore area and mainly do wedding photography. I have been looking for someone to partner with as I'd like to expand my business into wedding videography. I saw your posting offering wedding video services, and I was curious to see if you had enough free time to maybe film some upcoming weddings for me. I could offer you $1,000 per wedding, with a produced wedding video along with filming, of course.

If you're interested let me know. You can reach back to me here or feel free to call me at xxx-xxx-xxxx.

Thank you very much,

Jeff Williams."

Ben was in awe of the email. Up to this point he had only filmed a few weddings and he was charging those who did book him a few hundred dollars just to get any kind of extra cash. The fact that someone was willing to pay him a full grand for the same work seemed like a blessing. He instantly responded to the email to let Jeff know of his interest. After he sent the email, his hand was trembling in excitement, for Ben this felt like the answer to really make ends meet.

"I'm taking a shower, you coming?" Lily shouted from the top of the steps.

"Yeah!" Ben shouted back. The one perfect routine they would always share, at least most mornings was showering together. Ben loved getting to lather and bathe Lily and today was no exception. As they undressed Ben in his usual form quickly became erect and Lily would always enjoy pushing down on it and watching it bounce back up, like a child with a door stop spring. They bathed, sharing the flowing water back and forth so they could each get clean. Afterwards they ran downstairs in towels and made love on the white and black patterned Ikea couch, the same couch that they picked out together running around the showroom gleefully in sync. Long before the reality set in of what it meant to be truly independent, truly on your own with almost no safety net. While Lily may have always tried to stay in that land of bliss, perhaps jealousy or perhaps a sheer lack of empathy but Ben would be there to remind her of all the issues they were always facing.

What they would eventually have together was like speckled sunshine on an overcast day, you knew the sun was there somewhere but it never stayed out long enough to make a real impact on anything or anyone.

Lily II

I had a permanent crush and it was one I wish never took root. After that day with Ben, my naive heart knew exactly what it wanted, and that was him. I was too afraid or shy to confront him, so I attempted to move on.

What I would find out much later was that Ben actually asked my best friend at the time out first. She was seeing someone else, but told him about me and how I still liked him. She wasn't lying, but how hurt do you think I felt all those years later when I realized that I was really just a second choice for Ben back then.

We started texting again and he asked me on a date. We went for a picnic at an elementary school near where he grew up in Dundalk. He picked me up from my grandparents', and by the end of that picnic we were officially a couple.

I only remember the way he first started holding my hand because of how many times he would repeat the story back whenever we had fights. I was wearing a Pokemon hoodie and he was commenting on the Charmander that was on my sleeve over my wrist. He was intentionally pointing at it and then worked his way over to my hand, cupping it tight. After that, we looked at one another and smiled. It was pure and simple young puppy love.

That first year was an amazing time for both of us. Ben was graduating from high school and I was coming into my own with a solid group of friends that I enjoyed being around. He came to my birthday party the next weekend and bought me the newest Panic! At the Disco album. My family loved him and I can honestly say, so did I. He was so full of life and energy. It was nearly euphoric.

Unfortunately, though that year flew by in a flurry, and it was really college that changed Ben. Maybe I changed too, but from that point onward things would never be the same.

Drive

The challenge was set for the young team. Make a short film in 72 hours. Easy…right? A weekend full of sleepless nights was ahead for Ben, Hector, Mairo and Tony. These four young men made up the team for the competition.

The night that things started they were given their parameters. Each film must contain:

- A Pee Wee Herman impersonator
- The line of dialogue "You'll shoot your eye out"
- Three red balloons as props

With everything set in place, the core team members all convened at Hector's home for the night to come up with the story. Things moved rather quickly, as they knew the easiest location at their disposal was Ben's grandmother's home. After her passing in 2010, it was sitting vacant, still with many of her belongings inside.

Keeping this in mind, things soon went more into the horror genre for what they wanted to create. They had the spooky house, so why not make it a ghost story? So, it was decided and agreed upon. However, even with this small bit of knowledge, they still had to write the story as it would be filmed.

At some point, the film *The Grudge* was thrown out into the air. It would be a ghost seeking some kind of revenge. The next element was to keep it simple with a couple living together. Then things all fell into place.

Everyone left except for Ben, who ended up sleeping over Hector's house that night. They talked more about the film with an air of excitement.

As soon as they could get started that next morning, calls were being made to get some actors to help for the weekend. Mairo had a friend who dabbled in acting who would play the main lead and after getting countless denials from Hector for Lily to be involved, Ben gave up pushing the point.

Eventually, after exhausting a few other leads everyone agreed on Hector's sister to play the girlfriend and vengeful spirit. Now it was on to the home location which would serve as the set and lodging for everyone, at least as things ramped up for this lone all-nighter to come.

The team was coordinated, filming on Hector's Canon 7D DSLR camera. The shallow depth of field it was capable of was remarkable at the time and with the rented lighting they had from Towson University for the weekend, they were getting visuals that would hold up for many years to come.

The plan was to try to shoot in order at first, something which went pretty close to plan for that night. Ben was letting Hector and Tony talk over the visuals while Mairo was helping record audio. They would switch roles every now and again, but as things progressed, they all settled into what they felt most comfortable doing. Ben enjoyed the producing aspect. He wanted to get everyone in the room, but when it came to filming, he lost his interest pretty quickly. If he couldn't get the exact look he wanted right away, it was too frustrating.

What they didn't expect was a large storm to come through Baltimore that weekend, cutting away almost any planned outdoor scenes. By some fortune of fate, the only scenes that had an outdoor component were the flashbacks, for which Mairo took the two main actors at a nearby state park. Since the scenes were supposed to be sad, the rain only added to the depressing element.

For some sort of food, Hector's brother Stevenson dropped down later on with a feast of chicken nuggets, burgers and fries from the closest fast-food place up the road. This was a meal that Ben would normally scoff at, but the hunger was so bad that without second guessing it he quickly scarfed it down.

By this point they were filming downstairs in the always flooded basement addition of the home. It was filled with cave crickets and old tools left behind by Ben's grandfather, who died before Ben was even born. It couldn't have been dressed any better to match the unsettling atmosphere of the final piece.

Mairo felt uneasy the entire night, and Hector's sister had to stay in heavy makeup for hours on end before they were finally able to film her scenes.

"Ben, I saw a ghost, in that back room."

"It isn't haunted...I told you that."

"How do you know?"

Ben would look into that room many times that evening and, while the light did flicker at times, it was a symptom of an electrical system that hadn't been upgraded since the 1970s.

The night was turning into dawn, and there were still many scenes to be filmed. Lily had started helping with the makeup process earlier in the night and she was dead tired along with Ben. The two of them ended up falling asleep on the dirty dusty floor as scenes were quite literally filmed around them. The main actor was jumping over them as he attempted to flee the now locked-down home haunted by his girlfriend's vengeful spirit.

The storm had passed and the sun was shining that early morning. The final scene had the three red balloons lifting off into the sky as a visual symbol for the spirit finally finding some sort of peace.

A week later the festival screening was held. Four other groups participated that weekend, with two of those four presenting some strong competition. The final piece, which was intended to play like serious horror came out more along the lines of *The Evil Dead* slapped together with those classic J-Horror films of the late 2000s. It was campy, but had a strong ending and all the required elements didn't come across as forced whatsoever.

After the last film, the judges at the festival had to convene and little papers were distributed to the audience to vote for their favorite of the fest.

Twenty minutes of nervous anticipation later the host for the evening stepped up to the microphone.

"Alright everyone, the judges have made their decision. The best of the 72 Hour Film Festival here at Towson University is…*Spiritus* from Ben, Mairo, Hector and Tony."

An explosion of cheering lit up the stands as everyone in the group and all their guests jumped in a cacophony of excitement. The four young men rushed up to accept the trophy and, for the first time in all of their young careers, felt a great sense of validation for what they were trying to do in life.

Once the cheering settled down, they all returned to their seats. It was time to make the second announcement for audience choice.

"So next up is our audience choice winner for the night. The audience choice winner is…*Spiritus*."

Another jump for joy from everyone. This time not as large, but the fact that they were able to sweep the festival that year felt like a miracle. Sometimes when a production comes together it simply just goes off without a hitch. This was certainly the case with *Spiritus* which, through a series of the best accidents managed to work at every point.

The celebration led to dinner at a nearby bistro. All they could do was talk through the afterglow of the night. Combing through every bit of detail of what they all witnessed, what they all experienced. It was purely magical and a true pinnacle of Ben's filmmaking career that would not be repeated on such a grand scale. That youthful energy and bit of naive brilliance combined to make something that even now felt like a complete fever dream.

Only Lovers Left Alive

  Mr. Williams Jeff, as he preferred to be called, sat in a booth at the Panera Bread in Canton waiting for Ben to arrive. Jeff, through his years of photography experience, saw the value in arriving to things early, if at an obnoxious level. He had a half hour of time to kill, so he ordered a turkey club on wheat bread. He finished the sandwich while thumbing through his latest iPhone model, as if to show the world he was doing well for himself. Client emails would come in steadily, whether it was to receive photos from their event or for new inquiries. Even if Jeff was happy that he was managing a successful business, the world would not know it. Jeff had a great way of maintaining a deadpan look, simply breaking for shows of aggression.

  Jeff finished his sandwich and felt content. As he was beginning to daydream watching the soft rain tap on the window outside, he heard a quick notification tone come up. As he picked up the phone it was an email from Ben announcing his arrival. Just as quickly Jeff responded

  "Thanks Ben,

I'm in a booth near the entrance against the window. See you shortly.

-Jeff"

Now sitting in his car, Ben was too nervous to just walk in to Panera and try and find Jeff. Firstly, he had never met him before, so there was the obstacle of perhaps interacting with the wrong person. This was a mistake he'd made before which, while to some not a big deal, was quite embarrassing for Ben. Moving forward, the email or text method of getting a general location was the way to go. After a few times refreshing his email messages he saw the new one from Jeff and after reading a few times over carefully Ben took a deep breath while exiting his hand me down minivan.

Ben entered the store and immediately walked through the extended line of people waiting to place their lunch orders for the day. He used to feel bad not ordering anything when meeting at an establishment, but at this point he had had so many of these that it no longer fazed him. He took a few steps into the dining area and swiveled around, trying to see if he could spot Jeff. No one waved him on so he started to walk forward and Jeff looking up from his phone could tell this nervous young man had to be Ben. He gave a side smile, a gesture as best a sign of positivity one could hope for, and lifted his arm up, motioning to come over. Ben quickly approached.

"Ben?"

"That would be me," Ben responded anxiously as he took a seat across from Jeff.

"Nice to meet you." The two shook hands and Jeff slid his empty tray to the corner of the table. "Would you like something to eat?"

"Oh no thanks, I'm not hungry." Ben quickly responded, hoping not to raise a further insistence as he really couldn't afford the luxury of an ordered lunch given his current financial state.

"No problem, so I'm glad you could make it out. Let me tell you a little bit about myself. So, I'm Jeff Williams, obviously, and I've been doing wedding photography for about seven years now. I've been getting more and more clients asking about video too, and since I'm by no means a videographer myself I'm looking to bring in outside help that can take care of the video side of things. I saw a few wedding samples on your site; how many weddings would you say you've done so far?"

"I've done probably about ten or so, not a ton but I know the basic format of the day," Ben said cautiously. Although in reality it was more around two weddings to this point, with one being a family event that was hardly anything formal.

"Great, so you're looking to take on more work then? You wouldn't say you're too busy to take on gigs from me or anything would you?" Jeff inquired.

"Oh no, I can certainly handle the work load."

"Perfect, perfect. Well, I will say I'm meeting with one other person today but I think he might be a little too busy for what I'd like to have on my team. Oh, the thousand a wedding is good with you right?"

"Yes."

"Awesome, well it has been nice to meet you, Ben. I will send you an email with my decision this evening." Jeff again shook hands with Ben, gave another semi-smile and Ben left the booth just as quickly as he had arrived.

Jeff knew that Ben was probably a little green when it came to weddings but he, -wanted someone he could really mold into a permanent fixture in his soon to be further growing business. He looked back to his phone again, now regretting the gap between meetings he was going to have to wait through until his next candidate arrived. He thought about walking around but seeing the rain now pinging against the window even harder, this was a thought just as quickly dashed away.

Ben rushed through the rain back to the Chevy Lumina van that he had purchased from his parents. He affectionately referred to it as the space ship and simply going to a place like Washington DC for a gig would mean a refill before returning home. Every trip had to count and pay, as things were tight. Ben felt good about everything, his now sweaty armpits were proof of that in his mind, but he still would have to wait until the evening for an answer. Before he even pulled out of the parking lot, he pulled his phone out and wrote a quick follow up to Jeff.

"Mr. Williams,

Thank you so much for meeting with me today. I'm very excited to hopefully be working with you soon and if you need any more information, references, or anything at all just let me know. I've always been told I'm a hard worker and I know, if offered the position I will do my best to make every video up to your level of quality as I possibly can.

Thank you,

Ben."

The van started up with a quick low rumble and Ben pulled out into a busy Baltimore Street. The radio station was playing a favorite Fall Out Boy song of his and he sang along, hoping that this was a good omen for positive news to come this evening.

The Hunt

Ben sat alone in his room; he had been fortunate enough in his teenage years to reside on the entre third floor of his parents' house. He never really saw how lucky he was until he moved away. On this night, he was playing online, passing through the boredom. While in college for film, Ben was never really challenged at a level that kept his mind from wandering. Idle hands may be the devil's playthings, but a mind stuck in drudgery can create a horrible pattern of constant reflection.

This night, Ben received a message from an old high school friend, Moxley. Moxley was someone Ben would play basketball with (amongst other sports) after school. They were never super close by any means, but on this night Moxley did something better than any best friend could have done. He told Ben that he had seen Lily with another guy at a recent party he was at. He was one of the few people still in the area who knew that Ben was with Lily and in that circle of friends. It is an easy conspiracy to hold onto that Lily chose her circle for the fact that they were removed from so many mutual friends at the high school they attended. At that time, Ben would have completely believed it, but looking back now it was probably a convenient coincidence that made having an affair easier for Lily.

"Hey Ben, how you been man?"

"Pretty good, just hanging out, been a while, how's life?"

"No complaints here man. Hey, I don't want to intrude on anything but you're still with Lily right?"

"Yeah, we're still together. Hard to believe that it's been almost five years now."

"That's awesome! Well, hey, I don't know how to say this…"

"Whatsup?"

"This is between you and me man."

"Sure."

"It's just I was at a party last weekend over Bethany's and I'm pretty sure she was with another guy."

"?"

"Yeah, I mean I could be wrong, but like they seemed pretty close to me."

"Oh…"

"I could be wrong man, maybe you should talk to her but I wanted to at least let you know who the guy was."

"Okay…"

"His name was Gregory Kon. He has a Facebook; I can get you his profile If you'd like."

"Yeah sure."

"I'm really sorry dude."

"Don't be, I'm glad you brought it up, talk more soon, man."

"Yeah…it will all be good, man."

"Thanks,"

Ben clicked the link to the profile Moxley had sent over. He went over every post that Greg had put up, looked through every picture for any clues, Ben became a true detective searching for something more than just Moxley's word. He found nothing, despite repeated looking. He sat struggling with whether to friend request Greg or not. After careful consideration, Ben decided against it, noting that it might set off too many alarms, or alert Greg that he was with Lily. Instead, he found a phone number listed on his page. Ben wrote the number down and saved it in his phone. He thought it may come in handy one day.

For the rest of the night, Ben could not stop thinking about the possibility he was being cheated on. For Ben it seemed an impossibility, although he knew he was not perfect at all times to Lily, this seemed far too extreme an action on her part. His hands were shaking as he thought over what step to take next. He slept horribly that night, but did his best not to say anything to Lily, he wanted to get some kind of genuine proof.

Prisoners

The morning sunrise was an exquisite one despite the cold. Ben awoke to a message from Jeff asking him if he was free to cover a "training wedding," the following weekend, which he was. It was not a paid gig but at least the entry way into working for Jeff, one step closer to the thousand dollars a wedding Ben so desperately needed. Roxy ran around the rowhome courtyard as she did every morning. Today would be a long day, photographing junior league baseball games. Ben only made $25 a game and at most would get in five to six games between 8 a.m. to 6 p.m. Lily did not come home last night and Ben did not get good sleep because of it. She didn't text him back much, and his anxiety had ramped up.

Getting into the stadium to start the day at 7 a.m. was always so peaceful. Watching the fields have the tarps taken off and seeing all the families come in was a great piece of nostalgia for Ben. Although he didn't play many sports growing up, he cherished watching the close families full of smiles, if even for a little while. Baseball, he observed, was the great uniter, but it was something of a great divide, filled with fathers who took their sons' performance too seriously and mothers who simply wanted to socialize. Ben always hoped the wives of the short-tempered men would help them calm down, but they would either ignore the behavior or sometimes feed into it with their own words of anger.

When it came down to the actual job, though, Ben loved photographing baseball. When he would get a good action shot of a kid sliding into home plate or making a great catch, it would be a mini victory. He would feel like he was part of something bigger than himself and seeing teams play in the tournaments was great.

It gave Ben a new appreciation of the sport, one that he largely written off to that point. He would always tell friends that it was like exciting chess, watching the coaches tell the athletes something from the bench to counteract what they felt was an action incoming from the other team. It was all so coordinated, and when a team was good the amount of strategy, they would implement in order to try to win was really amazing. One piece of life that Ben always admired was how his career could take him to so many eclectic places.

The pieces of the day that Ben didn't like were having to get a team photo before the game. Most coaches would see it as something of an annoyance and often would find it funny to try to avoid doing it all costs. That is also to say that some coaches would downright get hostile toward Ben when he would ask. Ben was already shy as it was, -and any time he got a negative response it would cause him to not want to do it again. The worst piece of information Ben knew about these photos is that, each print a parent would buy cost $20, so the photo company would make their money back on what they paid Ben in the sale of two prints easy.

Some mornings, though, Ben was ready to take on the world and this sort of treatment did not bother him. This day it was the second of a multi-day tournament, so that obstacle was already covered. It was just about action photos all day; Ben was in his element and was capturing some great photos. It was cold, but the thrill of some good games kept things lively. It was a good day of $100 earned.

As Ben returned home Lily was still gone, he heard a little more from her during his shift that she was stopping home before she had work of her own. He daydreamed that he could see her for a little bit, but it was not to be. Roxy was in her crate and was ready to stretch her legs. The nightly routine was ready to commence again for Ben.

Julia

I just wanted to get high in his car, but he wouldn't let me. I mean a little bit of cocaine just to get me set before getting to the holiday party. I still remember that shocked look on his face when I asked.

"Do I mind if I do a bump off your dash?"

He just stared over at me like a deer in headlights. I don't think he had ever even heard so much drug slang in his life before. It was cute.

"I'll just do it in the bathroom when we get there." I think I said to him.

The job was some temp thing I worked over Christmas at this beauty place. Like an Ulta or something like that. I barely remember now. I do remember getting as much food as I could that night. I was starving. Ben didn't eat anything, though. He was a skinny little thing as it was, I didn't ask, but maybe he had an eating disorder or something. Not that I am or was judging it.

He seemed in a rush to get out of the room and was acting nice enough to some of my coworkers, even though he didn't have to. Trust me--with the guys I've dated, I've seen some pretty big--time assholes in my time.

I finished eating and we got these game cards and a free drink voucher. I wanted to take to the bar, but Ben was more preoccupied with playing games. His excitement didn't really peak until that point and he made a break for some dancing game. You had to hit the arrows in time with the song.

He loved it but I was bored pretty quick and wanted to do some kind of drugs…before I go on, let me just say, though, that I am not this way anymore. I am actually sober but this was just that time in my life where I was just doing anything I could get my hands on.

So, I left my jacket with Ben and I went to the bathroom. I think I popped a pill that night, some kind of downer, and next thing I knew I was out like a light. Just completely passed out. When I woke up, I can remember just hearing the announcement that they were going to be closing in a few minutes. I'm pretty sure I was knocked out for a good 30 to 40 minutes.

As soon as I walked out of the bathroom Ben was standing there with all our stuff. He got so mad at me.

"What were you doing in there!"

"Sorry...I was on the phone." I think was the excuse I came up with in the moment.

My preface to this next moment with Ben must be said, that I was again in a really bad place in my life at this time. So, for some reason, I made a confession to him in the car ride back to his place.

"I just wanted to tell you that I'm still seeing this guy on and off and together we snort heroin and smoke crack." I'm not proud of this moment but I had to tell someone, and Ben just seemed like an outsider I could share that with.

When we got back to his place, I remember he had these two neon heart lights on each side of his bed. He joked that it was his ode to the cheap motel look, but I found it kind of sexy.

We had sex for a long while that night. I can remember distinctly that he enjoyed having his nipples played with. I'm bisexual naturally so it was fun hooking up with a guy who was a little more on the feminine side.

In fact, I think he even played into that motif pretty heavy.

"Think of me like this perfect cross section of a boy and a girl." This was something I think I remember him saying that night. He was definitely a talker, which I didn't mind, but sometimes I just wanna get fucked, ya know?

He dropped me off super late that night. He said he had a video shoot the next day or something. After that point, I didn't really hear much from him for a while. I made sure to send him a friend request and gave him shit for not messaging me. His excuse was being busy, but that was just a convenient out.

After a while of some minor chats on Facebook, I decided to delete him as a friend. If I remember right, he sent me a request a few weeks after that point but I just deleted it.

The nice thing was that this was the night when I felt that I started to turn my life around. Ben may look back at it as something of a disaster date or a story he shares with his friends but I'll always see it as my positive wake up call.

Ben may not be a great person or someone that you could call all that remarkable, but he was a good listener, at least. For that, I guess I gotta give him some kind of credit.

Arrival

He pulled into the Woodend Sanctuary feeling a shell of complete isolation. His friends who were with him at some weddings were gone, Lily was long moved past their relationship, and he was stuck in someone else's fairytale for the next eight hours. When Ben parked the car, he stopped and sat. I could end it all here he thought to himself. He wanted to leave; he wanted the nightmare to end but he pushed on.

Looking back, he wondered in the young Asian woman and her family even noticed how bad he was phoning it all in. Maybe they would ask if I was ok, or show some sort of sympathy. Was that a selfish thought? Either way it didn't happen. He filmed her getting into her dress about as lazily as he could. The passion had been far past Ben at this point.

As the day drew on, all he could think about was his immediate family and all the things he was missing out on. Financially, things had started turning a corner for Ben, he had a business growing, but at what cost? His weekdays were filled with idle time waiting on the occasional client email or new lead, but his weekends were always booked out. All this carefree time that so many others enjoyed he was forced to spend working, and while he was free so many others were working the days away. He wished he could have spent more time with his sister, mother, father, even Roxy.

The ceremony was filled with eye rolling moments of words he had heard so many times prior. Any semblance of originality was completely lost into a void of searing darkness that engulfed every moment of the painful pleasures so many others smiled over. For Ben, it was as if he was in hell. A piece of him wished he would have left and forged a new career path, but the anxiety of what would come from a world of unknowns kept Ben transfixed into this world.

"I'm so happy I found you in my life. You truly complete me."

"Without your guiding light I don't know how things would have been for me."

All Ben had seen was a level of co-dependency he despised. He was jaded, after losing Lily to another man he wanted everyone else to be miserable. He couldn't believe that anyone would want to love in this place, but it was because of what he had gone through. Things were terrible.

As the day drudged on, the reception began and Ben filmed the speeches by selections of the bridal party.

"I can remember when we were little girls playing with dolls, we used to fantasize about how we'd find our own Prince Charming. You used to describe who that would be and you know what? I'm looking at him right now. You guys are amazing together and I love each day that we all get to hang out together. My only wish is that one day I can find someone half as amazing."

The bride would cry, the bridesmaid would cry, and they would exchange a hug. It all felt so predetermined, it felt like it wouldn't ever change. The saving grace of the evening was always when the dancing started. It meant that the dancing would start and Ben could get the basic amount of footage so that he could leave early. That was if they didn't have some kind of sendoff planned, like the dreaded 'sparkler waving goodbye' that only became popular after one wedding made it viral. Originality was not something that came along with this work.

A few weeks later the video was completed, and he sent the required finished DVDs to the couple. They seemed indifferent to everything and didn't really have complaints. If Ben was good at one thing at this point, it was how to charm his clients over email or by phone. If that was his only job, he would have maybe enjoyed it more, but alas, filming was always the one thing he had to do.

To his surprise, Ben would wake up to discover a new negative review on his company's page on Weddingwire.

"Ben produced a great video which we will cherish for a lifetime, but beware that he burns the DVD on a Blu-Ray disc which will not work in a traditional Mac computer, something I didn't know until after the fact. He also left the event earlier than he was supposed to, so make sure you clear the time with him first. 2 out of 10."

Much like the moment where he was sitting in his car contemplating whether to even film this wedding, he looked at the review with the same disposition. Was this a good sign to just delete his accounts and start fresh with something else, or was this a wakeup call to push on more?

Fool's Gold

It was the Fourth of July, and Ben was in the passenger seat of his best friend Hector's Infiniti G35. It was a holiday Ben spent away from his family, as tensions were still high as they had been for the last year. Ben and Hector decided to go to the movies, where they were going to see *Hellboy II: The Golden Army*.

The sun had faded during the drive and fireworks began to fill the skies. The late 2000s screamo and alt-rock music blaring in the car provided the perfect soundtrack to each crack of light emanating deep in the night sky. Ben found himself lost in the spectacle of each bang, feeling a sense of catharsis in a time of confusion. Top of the mind for Ben was his decision to go to college for Pharmacy studies. It was weighing on him especially heavy this evening. The movies were a pure escape for Ben and Hector.

"It's the peak of summer." Ben whispered. Hector quickly turned the music down.

"What?"

"July 4th, it is the peak of summertime, ya know? That time when summer has been going on and it is still too early to be worried of when school isn't coming around again."

"Yeah, I will always love summer nights, not too hot, but never getting cold."

The movie theater was a brisk thirty-minute drive from the small-town Ben and Hector grew up in, and tonight it wasn't very packed. They arrived early too, in order to get better seats for the screening. Ben thought back to the time recently where they saw *Indiana Jones and the Kingdom of the Crystal Skull* on opening night and got center seats at the top row, it felt like a great triumph. Tonight, was another night of small victories, as they were able to secure top row center seats. Hector had stepped away to get some overpriced chicken strips from the concession stand. Ben told himself he wouldn't eat anything, but Hector would inevitably offer one to him, which he would never refuse. Tonight, would be no different.

After the movie it was late, it was quiet, and the parking lot outside of the theater was much emptier than it was when they went in. For Ben, it felt like a somber moment after a bit of celebration. Going in, the fireworks were still raining from the sky, but as they approached the car it was strangely quiet. Ben was glad he spent time with Hector, but he felt ultimately unfulfilled by this decision. It was like he missed a moment of camaraderie with his community, family, or even strangers. It was as if he missed out on something that could have been more.

Before he could think too much, Hector began to run to his car for no reason except to do it. Ben started running too, knowing that if Hector beat him and got to the car first, he would lock Ben out while pretending to pull away. Tonight, it was a solid tie, and Ben was able to get in the car without much of a struggle, although Hector did get close to locking all the doors before Ben could grab the passenger door handle. It was a simple gesture but, whether Hector knew it or not, it kept Ben from overthinking things too much.

As they sat Hector started the car and pulled his Sony PSP from the center console. There was always a little delay between when the car started and when they actually began driving, as Hector chose the perfect song to start the drive off on. Ben would try to peer over on the screen to see what he was picking, but Hector always found it important to keep it secret, he had even gotten wise to Ben looking at the reflection of the screen in the window. Hector would always pivot his body to Ben so there was no way for him to see the screen. Tonight's selection would be "What happens if I can't check my Myspace when we get there?" by Attack Attack!

They made it back to Ben's home, where he knew they would sit outside for at least another hour or more just talking, it was routine but it was nice. They had just graduated high school, so talking about life with all the teenage drama that came with it seemed necessary. Ben and Hector could always just talk about anything for long periods of time, it was so natural. They would often wonder what it was they had even talked about the hour before as time wore on. Tonight though, Ben needed to talk about what he wanted to do with his life.

"I feel like I'm going to go insane if I do the pharmacy thing, man. Like looking at from a statistical stance, suicide is pretty high amongst pharmacists."

"What do you wanna do?"

"I don't know, I just see myself getting so burned out so fast, just spending my days counting pills."

"Yeah, I think that is a little beneath you man."

"I kind of think so too, but I don't wanna disappoint my parents, I want to do something that they approve of too."

"I get that, but you have to think about what makes you happy too."

"I've been really enjoying doing creative writing again, - it's been a nice outlet for me."

"Maybe something with that?"

"Maybe, but I don't know what career options are out there for that."

"You could do something with film, I mean I know I'll be out in Frostburg next year, but I'm going to apply to Towson for film."

"Yeah, they do have the film program there, I just can't do the pharmacy thing, the more I think it over, the more I know I'll hate it. Plus, we both know I suck at math."

"Just think about it then, do what makes you happy though Ben."

"I just need to act, and not overanalyze this. I'm going to do the film program."

"Fuck yeah!"

That night Ben went to bed happy, feeling like he had finally made a serious decision for himself when it came to college. It was completely set in his mind, he was going to go to school for film and the next morning he would tell his parents about it. They were reluctant but set that aside to let Ben follow what seemed to make him happy.

As Above, So Below

The note had been carefully hand written. Roxy was set in her crate and Ben left it on the table. He had a music video shoot today, a rare instance of creativity sandwiched between corporate video and wedding video productions. Days like this gave Ben a small ego inflation, enough to feel confidence in breaking up with Lily.

"Lily,

I'm giving writing this note not as something of ease for me. I wish things could have worked out but unfortunately the cheating has not ended, it has only gotten worse. I don't think things between us will work out, and I'm asking you today to please begin the process of moving out of this house. You legally have 30 days to do so and I am fine with this window of time of course. I'm not asking you to leave tonight, tomorrow, or the next day but within your best time frame over the course of the next 30 days.

I'm sorry things couldn't work out, but as much as I wish they could, they simply can't. We failed one another and I wish things could be different. Take this note as binding that 30 days from now you will be completely moved out from this house.

I'm sorry,

Ben"

With that, a span of seven years was to come to a close. It was a surreal feeling, and one that Ben in the moment did not give much thought to. He was tired of being unhappy and tired of finding reasons to stay with Lily. He knew that he was also to blame for the relationship failing, he could have done a lot more for her but the constant cheating he would not only hear about but outright see in posts from other men online was too much for him to bear. He left the note on the living room table.

The shoot was going as well it could, Ben was in the position he craved the most, that of control over so many elements of production. He did not rule with an iron fist or sense of arrogance, and he was actually very receptive of the creative team around him. His two go-to creators, Ryan and Mark, were also close friends. They had met a few years prior at a local 48 Hour Film Festival in Baltimore. Ryan and Mark actually won the competition that year and Ben was so impressed that he reached out to the two and they slowly became friends after Ben helped out on a production that they were working on.

As day turned to night, Ben would receive the first rumblings that the note had reached the eyes of Lily. His phone began to vibrate and he looked down to see who it was. Ben did not answer, partly because he did not want to deal with the confrontation at the moment, partly because he was trying to focus on collecting all the necessary shots of coverage for the final video. What started as a handful of calls turned into a frantic flurry of text messages from Lily. These would be harder to ignore, and during a short break, he looked them over.

"What was that note about?"

"Are you seriously just going to kick me out?"

"Pick up your phone."

"I fucking can't believe you, and you won't even answer my calls."

"I'm not leaving, this is ridiculous."

"Fuck you Ben, fuck this shit."

"Pick up your fucking phone."

Ben looked over all the messages with a cold determination. It was easy for him in his element, he had all the power on set and that would extend over to his life now. Even Ben was a little surprised at how easy it was to read over all these messages and not get worked up in the slightest. He simply smiled, feeling empowered, feeling a sense of control. As everyone got a quick bite of food, he texted Lily back simply.

"Refer to the note Lily. Thank you for understanding."

As anyone can imagine this did not sit over well with Lily. A mad dash of messages continued to fill up his phone's inbox as Ben went full speed ahead on the music video shoot. He did not mention it to anyone, did not lose the focus on the task at hand. Ben was determined to be the creative self he always craved to be and feeling a restraint like that of a dying relationship being so close to closure only helped in his drive. Ben felt like the underdog protagonist in his own movie playing out in his mind, this was his moment to shine, and he was going to have a new start.

As he pulled into the driveway, he was ready for a showdown but Lily's car was not in the driveway. He did not know where she went and frankly, he did not really care. The shoot was a success and he was accomplished. As he turned on the lights, Roxy's tail began waving back and forth, hitting the metal bars of the crate she called home. He let her out and greeted her with a flurry of pets as he slowly made his way over to the table. The note was virtually in the same location it was when he left. Lily had added to it.

"Ben,

Don't worry about me I will be coming tomorrow to get my things and then I will be out of your hair. I wish we could have worked things or you would have at least talked to me but I understand. I still love you and always will.

Lily"

Ben had read over her writing a few times. There was a part of him which deeply wanted to believe that she still had love for him, he was sure of it. However, he knew that the cheating had not stopped, maybe though they could talk it through. If she could make a solemn promise that it would stop once and for all things could be different. Maybe it could all become ok between them. As Ben laid down for the night, he placed his hand on Lily's side of the bed, now cold with an indentation that was sure to level out one day not far from this evening.

The Invisible Guest

A Friday night was here, a Friday night and after a week of not working it was the one-day Ben had a shoot. For tonight, it was to be a wedding.

As Ben drove down Eastern Avenue, he admired all the street lamps slowly coming on as the sun faded away. He was jealous of all the people roaming the city, going to bars, being with friends. He was wishing he could be one of them, one of the faceless masses in the crowd. The funny thing was that if Ben was not working tonight he would have more than likely just sat home watching TV or texting a friend.

He waited as long as possible to leave, until he knew he would get in just before being late. Ben was filming at The Four Seasons Baltimore tonight, a grand venue which he had been to before to film banquets and charity events. The fact that a family could hold a wedding here this evening meant that money was obviously not a problem.

Instead of getting valet, he parked at the garage next to the hotel, hoping that the company he was filming for would pay for that charge. As he parked the car, he had hoped to receive a message from Lily but nothing was coming in. Since the breakup, they had stayed in touch only over email. Ben was blocked in every other mode of reaching out.

It was never really clear why Lily stayed in touch or why Ben needed to stay in touch so badly. Looking back, maybe Lily was worried that if she didn't keep some channel open Ben would commit suicide, he had made mention of it before. For Ben, he needed to keep some kind of hope in his heart that maybe they could get back together.

The moment that his creatively driven confidence had subsided, Ben immediately wanted to find a way to get Lily back into his life. In as many attempts though, this would be something that would never come to fruition.

Staring at a screen that gave sign of zero messages Ben finally elected to get out of his car, waiting until the clock hit 6:30pm, the time he was designated to arrive. He was aware that a 6:30 start time meant he should be inside the venue ready to go, but he really did not care this night. He pulled out his camera and a monopod for filming, which was the least amount of gear he could possibly bring.

As he was walking in, he received a message from the lead videographer for the evening, Reggie. For Reggie, this was to be his final shoot period before moving to Australia to start a new life. Another notch of jealousy was resonating through Ben, for he felt that Reggie was doing what Ben had so longed to do, escape.

"You here? When you get in, come up to the second floor and to room 315. They have the ceremony space all set up and everyone is about to start taking their seats now. I will cover up front and you can hang in the back for the B shots of everything. If you have a longer zoom lens, go ahead and pop that on, see ya shortly."

Ben had on only one lens that he intended to use the entire night. It was his second oldest lens, a 24-105 which sat at an ok f-stop of 4.0. For a wedding, this was actually pretty terrible for many of the low light situations to come, something again that Ben was keenly aware of but did not care about. For his own laziness and ease of work, Ben opted to take the easiest route he could so as not to even be bothered to change lenses throughout the night. If it got too dark, he would simply crank up the ISO and all grain be damned.

It was a young Jewish couple who were to be married this night. Ben saw that they did not have a traditional chuppah at the front of the room, which signified to him that they were not super traditionalist or orthodox. It also meant the angles of the night would be easier because from the back of the room, working around the legs of the chuppah could be problematic with blocking faces.

Everything with the ceremony went fine and he did not properly introduce himself to Reggie until the few moments afterward when the guests were to go to a short cocktail hour. Ben didn't really care, but made his best fake happy attempt possible. Reggie either didn't notice or was too caught up in the night to care.

After leaving to get some shots of guests eating foods that Ben had never even heard of by that point in his life during the cocktail hour, he moved into the reception hall. The entire rest of the floor was laid out for this one wedding reception. What seemed like maybe forty or fifty guests quickly ballooned out to three hundred or more. The space was massive and provided another reason for Ben to overthink his own place in life.

The amount of money spent on one evening seemed to eclipse anything Ben had acquired by this point in his life. Each table had a beautiful floral centerpiece, fine china, multiple glasses for champagne, water, and wine. They had a complete nine-piece band and an open dance floor to accommodate almost the entire crowd. Each large pillar had up lighting, and an extra DJ was on hand to handle microphone duty for toasts and speeches. In the very back, on a large riser, there was even a painter on the ready to paint a complete original scene of the evening. It was an extravagance that Ben had flirted with at other weddings but on a night where he was already feeling so low, this was just too much.

Most of the night, whenever it seemed Reggie was too busy to notice where Ben was, Ben would be checking his phone, hoping to get a new message from Lily. In the in-between moments, he was playing on Tinder, hoping to connect with someone to at least make idle conversation with. Ben was distracted and depressed, where at first work helped to fill the void left by an empty home, the constant feeling of seeing people in what could be described as true love turned any amount of money made a seemingly fruitless endeavor.

Any time he could get away from the reception hall Ben did, walking back and forth to the bathroom, playing on his phone, or sitting down to a vendor meal-it all was taken. Even though he was filming for another company, when members of the band and other vendors asked about his company, Ben handed out his own business cards. He was at least honest it was for another vendor but did not mention them by name at all.

It was a taxing and grueling five hours that seemed to go by at a snail's pace. The speeches especially were once again one of the hardest parts of the night. Hearing these stories of success in life, love, work, etc. It all felt like a new stab wound to the chest, over and over, tearing apart the core of what made Ben feel any semblance of happiness.

Looking down at his phone the magic number of 11:30 p.m. arrived and Ben shook Reggie's hand. He wished Reggie luck with his new life in Australia and quickly made his way back to his car. A fresh charge of $25 for parking was added to Ben's debit card.

Making his way back up to Eastern Avenue, Ben peered down Broadway Street to see the crowds of people still making their way around the bars. He could have just as easily parked the car and walked about the crowd, as in many ways the night was still young. He felt tired though, and overdressed, an easy excuse to make in order to just get home. Any money spent at this point felt frivolous, and on top of everything else, Roxy was anxiously waiting for Ben to return cooped up in her crate, a fact that always made Ben feel bad.

As he arrived home that night, Roxy greeted Ben with a burst of energy as he unlatched the crate doors. Her unconditional love for Ben was one of the few things that always brought an instant smile to his face. They walked to the back door and as soon as Roxy could roam the backyard she did, tonight Ben joined her, running around blowing off the steam from an evening of contemplation.

A week later, in the middle of the night Ben received a message out of the blue from Reggie. It was a special request as the two of them were not friends, but he still got the notification from Facebook just as quickly.

"Hey man I don't know if this is something you want to do full time or not, but this footage you shot is absolute shit. I mean Christ, man, there is like 10 feet of fucking headroom in each frame. Have you even composed a shot before? This is unusable, and also as the last wedding video I'm going to be editing a complete nightmare to do. I mean I'll give you credit it is in focus but fucking A dude, this is pretty miserable stuff. I'm pretty sure you do have a company of your own and if you charge people for this kind of work, I feel sorry for them."

At first Ben read the message and went back to sleep, but over the next few days the lack of effort he had put in that night really sank in. He sincerely wished that this would be the last time in his life he would not let his own emotions cloud his work ethic, but sadly this was not to be the case. It was a small lesson, but not the complete one. Not quite yet.

Gravity

Tomorrow they were going to a concert. Zach and Heather had come over to stay the night with Ben and Lily. Lily had known Heather since middle school, and it made Ben happy that he was spending time with friends of Lily. The house had been free of fleas, and money was ok for the first time since Ben had moved away from home.

Zach and Ben sat at the couch playing *Streets of Rage I*, *II*, and *III* until it was time for Ben to try and get some sleep. Despite the concert the next day, Ben still had to work early in the morning, taking school photos for students at Johns Hopkins. He called it a night and left Zach, Heather, and Lily to themselves.

Lily and Zach went out to the front yard to smoke a cigarette. Ben had asked Zach to just talk with Lily at some point to make sure she was staying faithful. He knew that Lily would probably catch on to what Zach was doing, but he still wanted to see if anything was going on. As they talked, Ben slowly eased himself under the windowsill, sat and leaned up against the drab white painted drywall.

"How have things been here?"

"You know, good, Ben working too much as always and I've been at the Chili's up here."

"Cool, cool. Ben's been head over heels for you for a long while."

"I know, I love him too. How you been?"

"Good, things with Megan didn't go so hot, but you know how it is, back on the prowl now."

"Oh yeah, you'll get someone good, don't worry."

"I'm not. When you guys gonna tie the knot?"

"Psssh, I'm in no rush here."

The two finished their cigarettes. Ben had enjoyed his voyeuristic moment of listening in. It sort of turned him on a little bit. That flutter he got in his chest of whether someone would notice what he was doing was always kind of a rush for him.

He made his way back to bed and after a little bit was able to drown out the television and laughter coming from downstairs. A few hours later, Lily would make her way up to the bedroom. When she laid in bed Ben embraced her and gave her a long tight hug. They would not make love tonight, but Ben felt satisfied knowing that tomorrow they were going to have a fun day, even if he did have the barrier of an early morning of work separating the joy that was to come.

Ben did not dream that night but he slept soundly, he slept deeply, and for once he woke up wishing he could be lying next to Lily, enjoying the peace.

Lily III

Years two through four with Ben were rocky, to say the least. I can remember our first fight quite vividly. I was over his parents' house and it was something to do with another trip to my dad's house in Indiana. I was only able to go once a year, but Ben wanted me to stay so we could have more time together that summer. I couldn't just not visit my dad, and Ben was irate.

It shouldn't have mattered so much, but there he was, arguing for me to stay. He was trying to say something about going every other year but I couldn't let that become a thing. The compromise would have been to just have Ben come but something told me not to even suggest that. In seven years of dating, he would never come out with me to my dad's house.

After that, the amount of fights would become so frequent and over so many ridiculous things that there is no way for me to even come close to remembering them all. I just knew that the Ben I fell in love with was not there anymore. He was gone and something about his time in college changed him.

After we broke up, I had heard stories of him talking to other girls while at the university so I don't know if he had regrets that he wasn't single then, or if it was just a new pressure he hadn't experienced at our smaller high school.

Not that someone simply taking film school could be under that much pressure. Ya know?

This was also around the time where he and I had our first break up. He tried veiling the move as a short-term break, but I wasn't going to let myself be played like that. I knew from friends who had gone through that what it really meant. Essentially, Ben wanted to fuck someone else and then come back to me if it didn't work out.

When I didn't let that happen, the fight started and continued the whole way back to Ben's house. I guess he thought he could bring me over to just collect my stuff and go, but I just remember the amount of sheer yelling that day.

His friend Hector even made this nice poster for our three-year anniversary, which he tore down in a fit of anger. That was the day he slapped me, too.

I was so angry I threw an alarm clock I bought for him square at his crotch. It missed, but it still hit his hip really hard. He walked up to me in a fury and slapped me in the face. Naturally, I slapped him right back as hard as I could and stormed out of the room.

I refused to let him take me home and my mom picked me up. I told her what happened and in her maternal splendor she called the cops. They went to Ben's house but I didn't press any charges. I could have gotten a restraining order that day and, in hindsight, I wish I did.

I don't think I want to talk anymore about my time with Ben though. This story doesn't get to any better of a place for either of us. Seven years I wish I could get back, seven years that I wasted on some stupid boy.

Warm Bodies

The alarm rang at 3:30 a.m., as was usual for Ben, he had plenty of energy getting out of bed and taking Roxy downstairs to start his morning routine. This time he would have to be extra quiet, although with Roxy bumbling down the steps, it was fortunate that Zach and Heather were both heavy sleepers.

Let Roxy out. Set up dog food. Grab cereal bowl. Pour cereal in. Check on Roxy. Put bread in the toaster. Let her back in. Butter toast, garlic. Pour milk into cereal. Eat.

These were the regimented thoughts from Ben as he started his day. It was merely step one in a complex, multilayered program to get him ready to walk out the door. It was all sacred and required to start the day properly, and any misstep would send his anxiety skyrocketing. It was all contained in the stomach, if Ben felt even slightly uncomfortable in his gut, the day was off.

Things went smoothly so far, though, breakfast was actually the easiest part of this. For Ben, the act of pooping was actually more gratifying than getting nourishment from a meal.

Dishes. Checking email. Bathroom (forty-five minutes maximum). Usually, no time for a shower afterwards. Brush teeth. Quickly get dressed. Give Lily a kiss on the cheek. Out the door.

It was nearing 6:00 a.m. by the time Ben walked out the front door to make his way into Baltimore. He parked in the closest campus garage, which would cost $20 (to be reimbursed) by the large school photo company he had worked for. The other two photographers he worked alongside would always park on the street. It was closer but was metered, which meant that every two hours they would have to refill the meters (Ben was pretty sure it was an excuse to walk away from work for about twenty minutes, a move which would almost always lead to them being backed up on portrait sessions).

The Hopkins portraits were always a bit of a pain. With most school photo sessions, the kids are younger and they get a photo then move on. Since this was a college campus, the students were, of course, in their late teens and twenties. They were well aware that it was all digital and they always wanted to see how they looked. Time after time after time, Ben would have to hear the same initial reaction of derision from people he had taken photos of over the years. No matter what, the majority of people always hated the way they looked.

It was frustrating, the lighting was good, the backdrop was placed correctly, the way he would have them pose was good, but they just hated their picture. So instead of understanding that a photographer cannot alter someone's face, they would insist on another picture. Ben would be patient when this happened, he understood, especially when you'd have moments where a person blinked by accident or had a stray hair. Many times, though, this would not be the case; -in particular on this day, a young woman asked for her picture to be retaken a total of seven times, each with a pause in-between to look at the last photo. It became such a process that she began to syphon through pictures 2, 5, 6, etc. Each time she would complain of another small detail.

Ben stayed patient despite this, and in the end, she went with one of the earlier photos they took. Rather than giving Ben a thanks or some kind of acknowledgement of his extra work she decried that it was still just an ok picture, with it being the best of a bad bunch.

This always felt like an underhanded jab of Ben's artisan abilities. Was he a bad photographer? Did he do something technically wrong? Was he bad at showing off his work? These moments always stuck out the most to him because it made him feel like maybe he wasn't meant to do creative work like this.

Photography may have been the second fiddle to videography but he still wanted to do good in it, even in the world of basic studio style school photos.

After a long half day, at 1 p.m. they finally wrapped up. Ben broke his set down as quickly as he could and set everything on his cart that he shuttled all the way back to the campus garage. It was about a half mile walk from the building they were in.

He sent Lily a text and jetted home as fast as he could He was tired, but the energy and excitement coming from Lily in her reply kept him happy. In forty minutes, he was back in Edgewood, where everyone piled in the car to then drive down to the Patriot Center in Fairfax, Virginia.

It was a long drive but everyone expressed great thanks to Ben for making the trip down. They blasted Fall Out Boy and sang along to every album they could play before getting to the arena.

They were early, but it was already crowded with people. As they walked along Ben stopped everyone and delivered his surprise to Lily for the show. He splurged on Lily's ticket and was able to get her a VIP spot to actually meet the members of the band. She was ecstatic and nervous. She had to go to a different entrance and Ben walked with her to make sure she found it ok. When they did, she gave him a long hug, thanking him so much for doing it. It was an amazing moment for Ben, who had felt that in this moment all the troubles from the last five years could melt away, if only for just a little bit.

When the VIP meeting was finished, Lily returned to the main line with everyone else shaking, crying, exclaiming how amazing it was. She had met Patrick Stump, a singer she had idolized since middle school, and gotten her photo taken with the band. Ben just kept smiling and was happy that she was so happy.

The concert was amazing, of course. While the seats they had were not on the floor, rather high in the bleachers it was still a great view. There weren't many people in their section, so they all danced and sang along with every band that performed. The opening act was Twenty-One Pilots, followed by Panic! At The Disco, and lastly, Fall Out Boy.

Ben reveled in enjoying the music of course, but he loved taking time to just watch Lily dance along to the show. The lights hitting her face, illuminating her porcelain skin, and her endless smile. Although her teeth were crooked, it was always something that made Lily unique to Ben, and while many of his business friends would bring this up as a negative feature, Ben would never see it as such. For Ben, the happiness was not in what he was experiencing but rather seeing what the people he cared about were experiencing.

This was the kind of group contact that Ben wanted to enjoy more often, but on so many occasions would slip through. He would be working during the day, Lily would be at night. Given the fighting that ate up so much of their relationship, the times when either would have felt happy or ok enough to want to interact with anyone else was rare. This was a day where Ben made sure he would fight through any anxiety flare ups as best as he could for Lily, and Lily would be open to letting Ben in to see her friends.

As they drove back home, the mood in the car went from nonstop talk of all the songs that were played, the surprises of seeing Brendon Urie coming out to do a duet with Patrick Stump among others, and all the cool fans that were also there to one of somber, car-fueled sleep. Ben bought a denim cut off jacket and got Lily a new shirt from the merch table. Zach, while more of a fan of rap music still had a good time, despite only knowing a few songs overall.

When they made it home to Edgewood, they all said their goodbyes, with Zach and Heather driving to their homes for work they had in the morning. Ben and Lily were tired, but Roxy greeted them with a day's worth of energy, to which Ben let her outside as quick as he could open the back door. Lily immediately went upstairs to start the shower and Ben joined her as soon as Roxy got back in.

They made love that night, softly and slowly, half asleep but with the same passion they had shared in nights prior. If there was one thing that Ben and Lily would always connect on, it would be the sex they enjoyed together. Usually, it could go on for a few hours, but this night they didn't stop so much as they did peter out after about thirty minutes or so.

They cuddled up next to one another, bodies folded inward, and fell into a nice sleep. Ben would have the day off tomorrow, and Lily would not have to work until the afternoon. For a single day Ben felt secure in knowing exactly where Lily was without a worry of cheating, and Lily got her chance to spend time with an old friend while seeing Ben in the same charismatic charming state that made her fall in love with him in the first place.

The Call

The vibrating, pulsating alarm woke Ben to a world that was still pitch dark. Lily was sleeping soundly next to him, as if no noise had come at all. That always amazed Ben and he took a minute to look at her soft face as she slept. Her rhythmic breathing and jaw slightly ajar was so innocent. He didn't mind that she had a slight snore in her sleep, it was cute. If it wasn't for a fear of waking her from this peaceful state, he would have given her a kiss.

Ben had to get up in order to start getting ready, even a few minutes past his proposed wake up schedule could make the difference between on time and late. It was Thanksgiving today and like most days, Ben found himself having to work. Today was a special day, though, as he was selected from a roster of photographers at one of his jobs to photograph the prestigious (at least to kids of a certain class in the private school space) Turkey Bowl. This was a once-a-year football game played between Calvert Hall and Loyola Blakefield, two private Catholic high schools in Baltimore. This year it was played at Ravens Stadium and Ben was, for once, actually excited to tell friends and family about it. It made his otherwise feeling of a failed career so far seem ok.

As he was getting ready, he was actually ahead of schedule today, moving along at a nice pace. His bathroom time (as he called it) went well and he was getting himself dressed before heading back down the stairs to get some snacks gathered. As he did, he could hear Lily on the phone.

"Fine, we don't need to come over."

"We'll stay here, fuck it."

"Yeah fuck it mom, it's fine."

Ben slowly made his way down the steps. Lily let out a long exhale and flopped herself back down onto the pillow of the makeshift bed in the livingroom.

"What happened?" Ben asked with a concerned tone.

"My mom just said she didn't want you over today."

"Why not?" Ben asked without realizing the history of fighting that Lily's mom witnessed over the first few years of their relationship. Once things escalated so much that the police were even called. Ben would not have felt comfortable sharing the dinner table, but he wanted to try, since this living arrangement was meant to be a fresh start for the relationship.

"You know why." Lily muttered.

"Maybe we can try my parents' house?"

Lily did not want to but she agreed to at least try. Ben went into the kitchen to gather things before having to leave. He was at least going to try to enjoy the fact that he was going to photograph this football game today. He gave Lily a kiss and went out.

Arriving at the stadium was a bit overwhelming. Ben knew this was a game with history to it, but the immense crowd rivaled that of a regular national game. After finding his second photographer for the day they slowly made their way to the inside of the stadium, below the seating, to an area very few would ever see.

It was surreal seeing the bowels of this huge complex, where big time stars of the game would prep and practice. It felt good that a career choice like filmmaking somehow led to this moment, and it was one Ben was excitedly texting his friends about. In the midst of all this Ben sent a message to his mother asking about coming over for Thanksgiving dinner.

The game started and the number of media on the sidelines was more than Ben had ever experienced. He was used to having to be mobile to get good shots, but this was next level in that regard. The bumping and shoving was not intentional but rather part of the crowd that was all vying for a good photo, or some cool video highlights. Even in the chaos, Ben still got a few solid photos. Of course, with him being seen as a simple yearbook photographer, the expectation was pretty low. At the end of the day, only a few pictures would even make the final print and between two photographers, they were more than covered.

As halftime came, Ben had a moment to check his phone. Looking down through the missed messages he read the one returned from his mother.

"You are more than welcome to come but we would prefer Lily not be there." Ben was taken aback. Of course, given the history that was embedded in their relationship it should have been obvious, but Ben wanted this fresh start to be just that, a fresh start for everyone. However, even after a quick exchange the sentiment did not change. His family did not want Lily over.

Ben quickly called Lily to tell her before halftime was over. He was surprised that she was actually in good spirits about it all.

"Fuck em all, we'll just have our own Thanksgiving, we have our own little family here anyways."

As the third quarter drew to a close, Ben and the other photographer made the mutual decision to call it a day. Of course, they made sure to agree on what the hours would be on the time sheet. Flubbing it by adding an extra hour and a half pay which with the holiday rate wasn't bad at all. This was another time where Ben wished he could make that kind of money on a more consistent basis, if so finances wouldn't be so tight.

When he returned home Lily greeted Ben with a long hug. They had no turkey, barely any food in the fridge, and were completely unsure if the closest grocery store was even open. After calling it up they found it was luckily open for another hour. So, they rushed over and picked up the next best thing which was a pre-cooked rotisserie chicken.

Ben sauteed some peppers and Lily prepped the premade potatoes. It wasn't perfect, but it was something they could call their own. The chicken was dry, the potatoes were over seasoned with garlic, and the peppers were a touch burnt, but they enjoyed the meal.

For a single day, they were brothers in arms against their respective families, and it felt like old times. Those times before the fighting began, before the divisions amongst friends, and before the threats of break ups. It was like that magical first two years.

After dinner, they decided to watch cartoons together and eventually made love for a few hours before passing out. Ben would fall asleep first, as he again had an early start to the day tomorrow and Lily sat awake looking up at the ceiling.

Her phone vibrated and she looked at a message from an unsaved number.

"Happy Thanksgiving, sorry I couldn't see you today."

"Happy Thanksgiving to you too! I know, maybe next year."

"<3"

"<3"

Lily deleted the message thread and put her phone to silent. She needed to get to bed before Ben started talking in his sleep again.

The Company You Keep

It was a day alone at home today, just Ben and the pets. A day of reflection with no gig leads or distractions made, the situation more severe than ever. Days like this left Ben restless and he was finding himself back on Craigslist, at first to look for possible jobs, but on this day nothing of significance was on the screen reflecting back. The next place was casual encounters, a place of regret, a place of poor decisions.

Ben always justified his actions by the fact that Lily had cheated on him before, this was his innocent fun, his hall pass to act how he wanted. Plus, unlike his peering into the life of Lily every chance he got; Lily did not pay Ben the same kind of mind. It was like he always wanted her to but she never did, not once. If any indiscretions were ever found, it was something very obvious, in a way in which subliminally, maybe Ben wanted her to see.

The ad that caught his eye today was one he had stumbled across before.

"Looking for a male to play with me and my close friend. He loves to play and be played with. Bisexual guys are a plus, but it is not a requirement. Send stats as well as a pic. If we like you, we will be in touch."

Ben answered the ad the same way he had so many others, it was the same formulaic approach that he took to answering for gigs. Going through the sent messages in his inbox he copied and pasted the traditional response.

"Hey there!

My name is Ben, I'm 5 foot 10 inches tall and weigh 115 pounds. I am a skinny guy but with very good stamina. I'm open to all kinds of new experiences and can provide my cell if you are interested. I have attached a photo here for you as well. I hope you enjoy and look forward to possibly talking more soon.

Thanks,

Ben"

After this, Ben would attach a photo of himself naked but it was framed in a way as to not show his penis. It was as close as it could get without revealing it.

The day had moved forward. Ben didn't do much. He cleaned. He played with Roxy. He tried playing videogames, but it all seemed very blank today. As he was preparing dinner, the usual fare of a Lean Cuisine, he received an email.

"Hey Ben, thanks for getting back to us. Are you bi?"

This was the same response he received before when he answered the ad. Last time, he had answered truthfully with a "no" and did not hear anything back. Tonight, he was desperate to connect with anyone, so he answered the way he knew he had to in order to get an answer. He sent a simple "yes," in response. As he was eating, he received a new message with a number to text. He quickly sent a message and, after a quick introduction, that same number was calling him.

At first Ben did not pick up and let it go to voicemail. He was nervous about it all and was always just nervous with talking on the phone in general. Instead of leaving a voice message he received a quick message asking to call back. Taking a deep breath and with an overactive heartbeat he did just that.

"Hello."

"Hey."

"Are you down to play tonight?"

"Sure."

"Cool, and you're bi right?"

"Yeah, yeah."

"Okay 7:00 sound cool?"

"Yeah, I'm good then."

"I'll text you the address."

They hung up and a few minutes later Ben had an address to travel to on his screen. He immediately looked it up on his GPS and saw it was about twenty-five minutes north. It was 5:00 p.m. now, so he had to hurry up and complete his after-dinner bathroom time, shower, and get dressed. This new found motivation made everything a breeze tonight.

As he drove to the house, which was actually an apartment complex, he was nervous but also excited. It was the interaction he had been craving all day and, underneath it all, a secretive way to get back at Lily. There were a few moments where he contemplated turning around, but these were short moments that hardly deterred his mission at hand.

He pulled into the parking lot and sent the text over in order to get the apartment number. After a couple of minutes, just long enough to make him think he wasn't going to hear from anyone, a set of numbers, "128," appeared on his phone. He got out of the car and went inside, walking up a single flight of steps to see the apartment with the same numbers on it. He almost wanted more steps to go up in order to at least build up his nerves a little bit more.

He knocked.

A series of loud steps could be heard even from out in the hallway, the door rushed open and a woman who appeared to be somehow both younger and older than Ben opened the door. From an initial inspection Ben knew that she had at least a passing history of drug use, the jagged lines on the young face were always a dead giveaway. It was obvious, though, that even before the drugs entered this woman's world, she was not someone who was particularly attractive. Her breasts were of an ample size though, a body type not too distant from Lily's, which was always something Ben liked to see.

She grabbed him by the wrist and as soon as he was in the apartment there were three men sitting on a couch watching very loud gay porn. The woman took a minute to look outside the door as if to inspect for any police activity. This did not go unnoticed by Ben who realized that there was something more than likely illicit occurring inside the walls of this apartment. It didn't bode well for his own feeling of safety.

The three men on the couch, as if in some kind of hypnotic unison, all turned to look toward Ben. They robotically inspected him looking from head to toe before returning to watching the porn that was the on the large tv in the sparingly furnished apartment. The woman again grabbed Ben by the wrist and walked him quickly past the men.

They entered a dark bedroom where only a single light was on in the corner, providing just enough luminance so that you could softly see what was in front of you. The room had a red hue to it. She shut the door behind them. For a very fleeting moment Ben thought maybe the two of them would start making out or possibly just have sex. However, there was another person in the room, who Ben did not notice. He was sitting at the edge of the bed and stood up, catching Ben by complete surprise.

This was a tall, unsightly man who towered over Ben. He had to be at least 6 foot 5 inches or more. From the fractal of facial features Ben could make out he saw a figure that looked like a cross between Sloth from *The Goonies* and the human body Krang used in the *Teenage Mutant Ninja Turtles*. He was overweight with a large belly and he was wearing a tank top t-shirt. Not to mention the stench of body odor that quickly filled the room as he began to move even the littlest of bits.

Ben was baffled and now terrified of what was to come next. The woman had locked the door, and was standing directly in front of the handle. She introduced the man.

"This is Jeremy."

Jeremy reached out his hand and Ben, after a pause, shook his back. Jeremy did not say a word.

"What do you think?"

"What do you mean?"

"What do you think of Jeremy?"

"Uh…I mean I thought maybe we could have some fun."

The woman smiled to Ben. He did not know what to make of the gesture.

"Yeah, for sure, but I mean maybe you and Jeremy could…"

"What?"

"Well, you did say you were bi."

"Oh yeah well I mean yeah but sorry no offense he just isn't my type."

Silence enveloped the room and Ben thought this was the moment when his indiscretions were going to come back to haunt him. Given all the warning signs of the woman checking for police, locking the door, and this man who was clearly stronger than him, Ben thought for sure Jeremy might take what he wanted by force. Ben scanned the room as discretely as he could for signs of something that might be able to be used as a weapon.

Just as quickly the silence broke, the woman unlocked and opened the door. She grabbed Ben by the wrist and escorted him out. The three men had not moved and were still watching porn together. She opened the apartment door and pushed Ben out into the hallway. Before she shut the door, she left Ben with one final message.

"Lose my number."

The door slammed shut. Ben was visibly shaken; he knew he could have been raped by not only Jeremy but the three men in the living room. There would have been no way to fight off all of them at once. In an alternate timeline, these people took what they wanted out of Ben and he would have been completely powerless to do anything about it.

Ben walked out to his car, still processing what had just happened. What felt like the whole evening in reality only went on for twenty minutes.

As he drove away, he told himself that he did not want to take a risk like that again. In the next twenty minutes, he called a few close friends to talk about what happened. What had begun as a feeling of regret quickly turned into a story of glory, not unlike what a person who survived a battle in a war might reminisce about in a bar when they're half drunk.

The saddest piece of all was that Ben learned nothing from this. He never told Lily. He never told his parents. The next day he would be back on Casual Encounters, this time simply avoiding that ad.

Dunkirk

It had been three years since this feeling had bubbled up inside Ben, this feeling that someone might be able to fill that special spot romantically. He had been talking to Gabrielle for a few weeks and tonight was going to be their first date at World of Beer. Ben suggested it only because he had recently been there with friends so it felt familiar enough that at least any awkwardness with the first time going to a new restaurant was alleviated.

The theme of the outfit for this evening was red for Ben. He picked out a pair of red vans, with bright red jean shorts, and a white button up shirt adorned with slices of pizza printed all over it. His hair was properly gelled to the side and he made sure to shower right before leaving to alleviate any odor.

As he entered the restaurant, Gabrielle was already sitting at the bar. She had a great physique and was prettier than he thought he deserved. He didn't know if he was going to mess this up or not. The plan was to grab a drink and catch a movie after. Tonight, *Dunkirk* was the film they had in mind, at Ben's suggestion. However, Gabrielle left it with the caveat of a maybe. She did not want to commit to making that plan until they met in person and she felt comfortable with it. She had been on too many bad dates to want to waste another whole evening on one. Ben understood, but it made him even more nervous of messing something up and Gabriel leaving before the movie.

He ordered a whiskey ginger, and she picked out a local IPA.

"Why didn't you order a beer?"

"I don't really drink beer; I think I have a hops allergy."

"Then why'd you invite me to a place called World of Beer?"

"I don't know, I thought it was close to your place and I work around the area a lot."

"Okay."

Five minutes in person and Ben felt like he was already floundering, ruining this chance with this gorgeous pale skinned beauty he always had fantasies about. He scanned the room. On the screen in front of them was a broadcast of an Orioles baseball game. He jumped at the small talk chance.

"Do you watch baseball at all?"

"No, I actually kind of hate baseball."

"Yeah, I mean I watch it from time to time but it isn't something I am like really into or anything."

"That's good."

Silence entered the room again. It didn't help that the bar was almost completely empty. It was easier to be talkative with the noise of a crowd drowning out their conversation. Being the only talkative party in a space, their conversation echoed throughout the room. Ben knew he was being paranoid by thinking anyone was even vaguely listening in, but he didn't like the fact that people around might be.

"Well, so you're from Atlanta, right? Tell me more about what brought you to boring old Baltimore?"

"I traveled all over, I was in school for architecture but it was overwhelming so I left and sort of just went on a few journeys to different places. I was a flight attendant for a while and a few of my friends from Georgia moved up here and so I figured, what the hell. I've honestly only been here a few months now so it is all still kind of new to me."

"Are you working anywhere locally?"

"Yeah, I'm at the Sagamore Pendry Hotel in Fells, it's a pretty cool place, except when I have to leave at night, I hate it then."

The conversation flowed finally with ease after that. They chatted for another thirty minutes or so, and Ben brought up the subject of seeing the movie. Gabrielle agreed, and he purchased the tickets for the both of them.

As they ascended the staircase to the theater, Gabrielle thought it an odd choice that Ben decided to take her to a war movie of all things.

"Why *Dunkirk*?" she asked Ben, who was just about to hold her hand. He was caught off guard, so he back-pedaled.

"I didn't want to waste money on any bad films, and this is supposed to be really good. I try to just see films that I think will have a solid potential for either enjoyment or artistic value."

Gabrielle felt satisfied by this response. Much like her own passion for architecture she could tell there was a passion for the art of film in Ben. It was a sweet sentiment.

During the movie Ben finally summed up the courage to hold Gabrielle's hand. As he did, she looked over to him and smiled. She leaned over and whispered in his ear.

"I was wondering when you were going to do that."

As they both turned back to face the screen Ben had a big smile on his face. This gorgeous girl seemed to be really warming up to him. In the time since his breakup with Lily, he had gone on dates, but nothing seemed to be as compelling as this. It seemed like the first sign of an escape from the torment of his own lack of letting go of that previous relationship. Gabrielle started to become a symbol of the escape from his own mental prison.

After the film, Ben walked Gabrielle to her car. The two hugged, but Ben did not feel confident enough to give her a kiss. He was, however, feeling bold enough to ask about a second date.

"So do I pass the test and get a date number two?"

"We'll see."

"We'll, see?" Ben mirrored back with overdramatic flair. It echoed along the parking garage.

"Yeah, I'll let you know."

"Okay."

The two exchanged another hug and Ben had a sudden flash. He remembered he was going to a concert in a few days and had an extra ticket handy. He turned around before Gabrielle could enter her car.

"Oh, I've got an extra ticket to see Alt-J next week. Did you want to maybe come?"

"Hmmm, sure."

"So, I do get a second date?"

"Damnit you got me…" Gabrielle and Ben laughed as she got into her car. Ben walked back to his car and drove home.

It all felt so right, it all felt so perfect.

Parasite

The wedding was to be held at the Sagamore Pendry. It was to be an elaborate day with over two hundred guests and a live band. It was a Jewish wedding, and Ben was to film from noon to ten that night.

It was almost a year since Gabrielle moved out, to go back home to her family in Georgia. They had wanted to make something long distance work, but Ben felt his roots were firmly planted in Baltimore. That, along with his own anxieties of being in a new location, were too much. He had stayed and she had left, and now he was filming back at the place she was when they first met.

Upon arriving, Ben had to use valet parking, something he wasn't sure if he was going to reimbursed for and something he knew wouldn't be cheap. He was early, and sat in the lobby surveying the people coming and going. He noticed those who obviously had money and also those looking to just party. Too many girls with very revealing outfits were still hanging on the arms of tired-looking men. The clashing of those indulging in their youth against the old stuffy well-to-do types was a fascinating dichotomy.

It was 11:50 a.m. Ben waited ten more minutes before hitting the button on the elevator to go up to the ballroom. It was ten minutes more than he wanted to pass. If he could freeze time completely, forever, he would have gladly done so. The nerves to just walk over to the elevator alone were biting away with each passing minute. Once the first dive into the water of the day was over, it would be fine, but to get to that point seemed as suicidal as a synchronized dive team jumping into a frozen lake. It was just too daunting.

The time came and Ben grabbed his cart of gear. He went all the way up to the ballroom level and instantly ran into the coordinator, who was stressing over the layout of the reception room. She seemed inexperienced to Ben and brushed her off for the moment so she could tend to questions from the florist.

The room they had set aside for the vendors was a small one, maybe a sixth the size of what the ballroom was. Ben took his time getting his gear set up. The photographer hadn't arrived yet, so he knew there was still some time before going to the bride and groom suites to film "getting ready" footage.

The coordinator walked into the room and the two photographers were with her. They were a female team; it was always a team. At nearly every wedding Ben filmed, he was almost always the only videographer, while there were two photographers. Most of the time, this was because the budget for photography was always higher than video, an old stand out from the days of film. The cost of entry for photography was cheaper than ever, thanks to widespread use of digital imaging, but somehow the prices never dropped off like they did for video.

They had to have a special key fob in order to even get on the floor with the bride and groom, which the coordinator had. She let them down and off they went to the suites. This was the part of the day that Ben was always okay with. He could now simply follow the lead of the photographers and just film from the background. He didn't have to interact much with anyone, just sort of follow the flow.

The bridal party was large and the suite was just as big to match, double the size of the vendor room if not a little more. They had been drinking mimosas all morning, the usual flumes adorned with everyone's names. Tacky and repeated a thousand times now to Ben. They all wore matching robes, again with names on the back.

The bride's mother was more stressed than the bride was. Perhaps it was the fact that she and her husband were paying for the majority of the day or that she was living vicariously through her daughter, but she was a train wreck waiting to explode at even the smallest out-of-place detail. These kinds of moms always made for a bad time, for you have to fight against them to keep the bride happy. You're basically a therapist keeping the thin strings attached for the time you were hired to be there.

Despite all this, things had run pretty smoothly, the bride was only slightly behind schedule, but the bigger issue was the whereabouts of the groom. The secret was kept from the bride but, as reported on by the second photographer, only the groomsmen were in his suite, with the best man missing as well. They were apparently procuring booze from the closest liquor store across the street from the Pendry. In any case, he was not present to get *his* "getting ready" photos or video, and Ben was left just filming the same few people sitting in the makeup chair, waiting to hear when the groom was to get back.

This was not to be today, though. The bride was in her dress and ready now to do the first look. It was far past the time for prep coverage. The groom was finally found somehow, at the spot of the traditional "first look." He was hammered. Drunk to a point of complete and utter obnoxious debauchery. Ben had seen couples getting drunk at other weddings, he had seen a groom spend the whole reception vomiting in the bathroom from drinking too much. He had seen a bride being held up by her parents as she puked up her guts as he was trying to say his goodbye for the evening.

It was different this time, though. We weren't even at the first look, still at the beginning of the day, and this groom was already spoken for. All of this while he still had a drink in his hand.

"Is this the part where I get to see my soon-to-be-wife?" The groom slurred.

"Of course, now let's just set this drink to the side." The photographer said with a fake smile, grabbing his drink away.

They placed the couple and had the groom stand at the top of a grand staircase as the bride walked up behind him to tap him on the shoulder. The groom gave her a kiss.

"Are you drunk?"

"I've had a little bit. You know, just to take the edge off."

The bride was already embarrassed. She looked over to Ben and the photographers, apologizing. It was too bad the day was only just beginning for everyone. Next up on the agenda was the bridal party photos. Corralling twenty adults in front of the Pendry at two in the afternoon on a Saturday. Keep in mind that this is situated in front of a busy Fells Point main street where cars are constantly buzzing by. What did the bride have on her list of photos but a request that they show as few cars in the background as possible.

Somehow, miraculously, the groomsmen had, during the short time of being left in the groom's suite and arriving outside had all managed to kick back a few shots. They were almost all completely drunk, now too. With each passing vehicle giving a congratulatory honk, the men hooted and hollered at the top of their lungs. The photographer did her best to yell over all the noise pollution but she was no match. She would confide over their short break at the reception that they maybe got two good photos during all of this.

The next step was family photos before the ceremony. Now the groom's parents would have the misfortune of seeing their son in a drunken stupor. It did not phase them, though. They behaved as if they had spent thirty-three years of his life to that point just tolerating the terrible behavior and ignoring it altogether. The bride this time had one request for the location, which was the Pendry pool. It was too bad that the pool was open to the public on a hot summer Saturday like this one. Trying to frame out the bystanders proved to be a difficult task for everyone. Combine this with strange pairings of people crossing between both families in a disorganized list, and again it was disastrous.

The drinking did not stop and in order to calm the bride down, the bridal party began making drinks for her as well. The groom was now in the phase of having a strange fascination with the genitalia of his groomsmen. Constantly grabbing at their crotches and squeezing their butts while saying he was messing around. In retrospect, he probably had his hands more on them than he did his own bride, at least until the reception.

They signed the Ketubah with the rabbi who was officiating the wedding. Ben had to run ahead of everyone in order to get a microphone on the officiant. With all the noise from the crowd, there wouldn't be any other good source of audio from the signing. During and afterwards, they were giving the groom just water at this point. This was to be short-lived, though.

The ceremony was fine, albeit cramped in the part of the Pendry where they have a large stone horse in an atrium. It seems cool from an aesthetic perspective, but in practicality it was far too narrow of a space, so trying to fit a camera on a tripod left Ben with few angles to pick from. He essentially had to finagle it, half on a raised planter and the other as far away from the aisle as possible. It worked, but it was not great.

Cocktail hour was always the boring time for filming. Everyone always just eats glorified appetizers and has a tendency to just stare directly at the camera as Ben walks by. Then there is almost always one person fascinated by the equipment. Asking questions about the cost and mentioning how they are an amateur videographer on their own. It wasn't that Ben did not like these people, but it was something that ate up time that could be spent setting up further for the reception or taking a breather.

When Ben returned to the ballroom, the band was finished setting up. They were six strong, with a dedicated sound operator. He got Ben a feed into his soundboard through an XLR input, which was always the most ideal way to go. Ben was happy, as this process was a simple one and the feed was good. Nothing slowed time down more than a DJ or Sound Op who couldn't get a good feed over to an audio recorder or who just had a bad system. Usually, in the secondary cases (if anything went wrong), it was always because of Ben's recorder, not any of their own faulty equipment.

The ballroom was filled with people. What once seemed to be a huge space was now packed in at almost every inch, leading up to the open dance floor. An extra tripod sat in the corner while Ben manned his gimble camera. The groom was only more inebriated at this point. The photography team mentioned this in jest while Ben was standing and waiting for the grand entrance of the couple. The lead singer grabbed the mic.

"Are you folks ready for this?" The crowd cheered in jubilation.

"Aww now what was that everyone? I said are you folks ready for this?" Now even louder, the noise reached a fever pitch.

"Introducing for the second time today, Mr. and Mrs. Schwartz!" The band belted into a jazz infused frenzy. The doors to the ballroom swung open and the couple waved out to the crowd as they clapped furiously. Ben stayed focused on them, walking backwards, tracking all the way to the open floor.

After the fanfare died down the band played the song for the couples' first dance together. It was *Kiss Me* by Ed Sheeran. A song Ben knew the lyrics to and actually enjoyed singing along to as he filmed the happy couple.

They finished their dance and again, everyone was cheering. Afterwards, the band took a quick break as the salads were served. The plan now for the photographers was to get the couple outside for sunset photos together. Unbeknownst to everyone, the bride, in her frustration of her new husband had taken some drinks herself during cocktail hour. In what was to be the last main job of the night both the bride and groom were lost to inebriation.

As they walked out of the ballroom together the groom began to talk with Ben.

"You don't talk much, do you?"

"I do, but I guess I'm just focused on the task at hand."

"That's a good man, but don't forget to have a little fun too." In a synchronous moment, the groom slapped his hand against Ben's butt. An innocent enough gesture in Ben's mind as they hit the button to call the elevator to their floor.

As they got off the elevator, the groom was now having trouble staying on his feet, so he began to lean against Ben in order to stay balanced. Ben now had the task of keeping the groom up while also holding his gimble.

"You're a good kid, you're gonna go far in life, ya know that?" The mix of various alcohols emanating from his breath crept deep through Ben's nostrils. All of this, combined with various hors d'oeuvres, snacks, and a few bits of salad assaulted Ben's gag reflex, which he could barely keep contained.

As they walked outside, the sun was hitting magic hour perfectly. The cool breeze from the water was a source of great relief. The photographers were in a hurry, the bride was right behind, calling to her husband to catch up. He was still leaning against Ben and soon his hands were reaching down Ben's back to his butt. At first the defense was some slight laughter while pushing the hands away. However, there was a persistence in the action, one that continued on and on. With each step ahead everyone else got, the longer Ben knew it would be before the groom would stop touching him.

"I'm just kidding, don't be mad boy." The groom sad with a sideways smile. His hands continuing down the back over and over. It was almost like a repetitive dance at this point. The groom found it nothing but amusing while Ben began to fade away from where he was. The body was on that pier in Fells Point, but the mind was overhead, lifted above, looking down helplessly.

The words the groom was saying turned into mush. Everyone was at the end of the pier while they were still a few steps down the length of it. That is when the dance stopped. The rhythm broke. The groom took away from leaning on Ben. The mind could now return to the body.

"I'm sorry." The groom said now standing in front of Ben. There was not a word exchanged after that. The two began to walk down the pier, now simply side by side. It was over.

"Honey, look at this view. Come on let's get our pictures." The bride called out in a drunken bliss.

"Of course, love."

The groom stuck his hand down as if to itch on the side of his leg, Ben still standing relatively close beside him. As the groom started to walk away, his arm swung back and his hand cupped over Ben's crotch. He took a quick firm grab only to then join his bride for their photos.

Ben stood there, astounded at what had just happened. No one saw it, their view too focused on the framing of the shot. The bride looking out to the water. Ben wanted to retaliate in some way but this was not his client, he had been hired as a contractor for this work. He bit his tongue and the mind left the body again for the rest of the evening.

As the night concluded, the photographers and the groom invited Ben to the afterparty they were having in one of the hotel rooms. Ben nonchalantly told them that he had another gig the next day and had to leave. He collected his things, placed them on his hand cart, and took the elevator down to the lobby by himself.

The elevator was adorned with mirrors. Reflections of Ben stared back at him as he thought back on the dreadful day.

As if to burn one last memory into Ben's mind, the groom gave him a wink right before the elevator doors shut.

As he walked through the lobby, two girls approached Ben. They both were acting erratically, overstimulated. Ben thought maybe they were prostitutes or call girls about to go to the afterparty or something.

"Do you like to party?" The girl said stopping Ben dead in his tracks. With the other girl right next to her it was a small barrier blocking Ben from reaching the exit.

"What?" Ben stepped around them.

"I said, do you like to party?"

"I mean I guess." Ben gave his valet ticket to the concierge as the two girls followed him outside.

"That's good, because I do, and my friend here does too. You're cute."

"Thanks." Ben looked around at the crowd, all gathered waiting for what were to be much fancier cars than Ben's own Toyota Prius.

"Do you have a phone?"

"Yeah."

"Can I see it?"

"Why?"

"I'm gonna give you my number."

Ben took out his phone and the girl grabbed it from his hand. She quickly typed down a cell number and saved her name in Ben's phone. They both walked away.

The valet pulled the Prius up after a few more minutes had passed. He offered to help Ben load his equipment but Ben told him not to worry, besides he knew if the man did help it would be more reason to ask for a tip which Ben did not have any cash for.

After getting back home and loading everything in, Ben sat in the living room of his home looking down at the number he was given. He almost deleted it but out of morbid curiosity he sent the girl a message.

"It was nice to meet you tonight, sorry I couldn't stay out. Maybe next time."

Only a brief moment had passed before the notification chime went off on the phone.

"Hell yeah, cutie pie, hope to see you soon."

Heather

I always knew that Ben liked me, all throughout high school. We would always have lunch together in our history teacher's classroom where we do nothing but share conversation about fellow classmates or just dumb banter.

I always loved his impersonations of various characters from *South Park*, including Cartman, which he was always more than happy to do. We never got too serious, though, with the topics. Always just light in our tone together.

After high school, we didn't really talk too much. I stayed away from the migration over to Facebook after Myspace began to die out and we didn't exchange numbers. It's funny how when you're in something like high school, you never think you are going to ever be that distant from your fellow classmates and then you just all of a sudden are.

Anyway, when I did get a Facebook page, we connected and he started talking to me again. It was light at first like old times but he started talking about how much he wanted to break up with Lily. I gave him my simple answer which was to just do it if he wasn't happy.

He tried, but couldn't go through with it, and after a little while of talking I agreed to see him one night. I knew very well that he was still seeing Lily and what ended up taking place that night was nothing but a lot of pleading for us to start dating.

I liked Ben but I never saw him as anything more than a friend. He just wouldn't give it up that night, though. We went through this same pattern of him bringing it up, a long-winded series of no answers from me and then awkwardly watching TV. He would break the silence and again the same cycle would repeat itself.

Mercifully, he would eventually give up, but even when I left, he still gave me the whole 'think about it' speech. Something I knew I wasn't going to do because I had already made up my mind. I'll never understand why some guys just think it is okay to do that.

Ben was a nice guy, but that sort of behavior just wasn't alright. Add to that the fact that he was still with Lily, and it just didn't make any sense to me.

The last time I would see Ben in any capacity relating to dating would be about five or six years later on Tinder, where I was just trying to have some fun of my own after a long-term relationship fell apart.

I honestly thought about it for a brief moment as I knew he swiped right on my profile, but I just couldn't go through with it. I still saw that guy sitting on his parents' couch begging me to basically be the second fiddle to his girlfriend, and I just couldn't ever let that go.

Ex Machina

It was a Tuesday night, a warm Tuesday night. Zach had come over to hang out as Ben set up a small bonfire. The constant dropping of limbs by the old trees in the backyard gave an almost endless supply of wood to burn. Ben had made a good habit of just making bonfires to pass the time when Lily was gone in the evenings. Zach had the night off though, so Ben invited him over.

Tonight, Lily was going to be getting off work early. As a result, there was only one thing that kept coming up in conversation between Ben and Zach, which was of the near three-way they had only a month prior at Zach's house. It was of course the brain child of Ben, who thought it might be something to appease Lily, as it would allow her to experience other men but with Ben. In fact, it had almost become an aphrodisiac for Ben who found himself asking Lily to tell him about her unfaithful sexual encounters while they had sex.

The only reason the last attempt at a three-way failed was at the hands of Ben, who was so turned on by watching Lily make out with Zach he came almost instantly. It had taken Ben by complete surprise, as his usual stamina allowed him to have sex for hours if the time allowed for it. He just had a good way of keeping himself from finishing, which was a skill that would later turn to a frustrating curse for the women who would eventually not enjoy Ben's stubborn refusal to finish.

Ben made sure to give Zach a few drinks, and Lily had mentioned she was able to sneak a drink or two at work that night in their messaging. Ben had a good feeling that tonight was the night.

Almost seemingly out of the blue Lily walked into the backyard. Roxy excitedly greeted her at the door, a feeling that Ben mirrored by jumping up to give her a hug and a kiss. Lily always gave such comforting hugs.

"What are you losers talking about?"

"Ah you know stupid shit as always, Zach's probably drunk."

"Am not, but I'd like to be." Zach retorted motioning to show his beer was empty.

Ben kicked out the fire and everyone made their way inside, walking through the constantly musty extension built on the house by Ben's grandfather. The never-ending leak that plagued the basement filled the entire room with a stale humid air that was always at its worst in the summertime.

Lily and Zach both took beers from the fridge as Ben filled his glass with water. They said a quick "cheers" and stood silently for a moment. Lily was the first to break the silence.

"Now what?"

"I don't know, I didn't get that far. I smell like smoke so I'd like to get a shower."

Ben walked from the kitchen to the main bedroom. Lily followed him and Zach was not far behind. Ben knew that if he had mentioned going to the bedroom than the charade would have been up, but in underhandedly leading everyone to the room there was a mutual decision everyone was making, whether they knew it or not.

Lily and Zach entered the room, each of them taking a spot on the bed. Ben was excited but genuinely did want to take a shower. Hygiene before sex was always important to him and he never wanted to smell bad. Especially if he was getting a blowjob, he would always feel bad for his partner, knowing that there might be a bad odor coming from his crotch.

"Well, I'm gonna take a quick shower. Lex, do you need to or anything?"

"Nah, I'm good."

"Well, I'll be back."

"Okay."

Ben made his way over to the bathroom.

"Don't do anything silly while I'm gone."

With that, Ben opened both the bathroom door and the door to an evening of fun he hoped to have unfolding as he entered the bedroom. He had this fantasy that would play out in his mind when he masturbated of walking into a room where Lily and Zach were making out or maybe even having sex. Without saying a word, he would just join in.

After his shower, sadly this vision did not come true. Instead, Ben made sure not to get dressed in the bathroom, walking into the room with just a towel on. Lily knew what Ben was really trying to make happen, so with that she made the decision to bring up the ill-fated three way from before.

"Remember when we almost had that three way? Maybe it's the booze talking but…"

That was all Zach and Ben needed to hear. Soon Lily was taking turns making out with Zach and Ben. They were both running their hands up and down Lily's body while she was rubbing both of them down, grabbing more and more at their erections.

Everyone got undressed and Ben was the first to penetrate Lily as she laid back, giving Zach a blowjob as best she could, contorting her body to give herself more leverage. Ben was about to finish again, but did his best to hold it. He switched with Zach as Lily began to suck him off, while he looked on seeing his girlfriend of six years take in the erection of another man. There was no going back now.

Ben couldn't help himself and he finished not too long after this. However, he knew this time he had to come back. So, for a little bit Zach and Lily had sex as he caught his breath, hoping to win back his stamina at any moment.

After a little bit he did and now there was no stopping him.

What had begun at midnight, now turned to two in the morning, 4 in the morning, 5 in the morning. Time seemed to just pass quicker than ever. Ben and Zach taking turns penetrating, getting head, penetrating, getting head. They knew when to switch and Lily welcomed it all.

In the final hour Ben and Zach both presented their hard cocks to Lily as she sucked one off while stroking the other, repeating this until Ben's foot touched Zach's by accident. It was as if a line had been crossed unintentionally, and now it was Zach who was winding down.

It was 6:30 a.m. when Ben and Zach had enough. They all were laying in the bed when Lily uttered words that Ben never thought he'd hear.

"Are you finished? I could keep going if you guys want."

It was so casual, so unassuming, as if this was a nightly occurrence for Lily. Of course, even to this very day Ben carries his suspicions of how often Lily would cheat but to see this unquenchable sexual side to her was something unseen for a long time.

Even if Ben had not been finished, this moment brought him back down from his blissful high. Instead of being an outlet, this seemed to spark a curiosity in Lily. For Ben, now the fear was to go from one man to multiples that Lily might choose to be with. He had opened a gate that may or may not have been crossed by Lily before, but at least now she had the experience of it all.

What had been a curiosity, a blossoming fetish, became a new place of worry. For if this did not provide some relief or change in the adulterous behavior, then Ben knew there was no coming back from it. If Lily wanted other men, then she could have that, and he showed her she could.

It was not as if Ben hadn't enjoyed himself too, but the goal was to give Lily her cake that she could now eat, too.

Ben walked Zach out front to his car. The two didn't say much besides acknowledging how the sun was starting to rise. Lily waved goodbye from the window in the bedroom as a new silence came over the house.

Ben went to the bed where Lily had already pulled the sheets over herself. He held her tight as they slept in until that afternoon.

"Could you really have kept going?"

"Yeah, I mean I orgasm but I don't know, I can just never seem to get enough."

Ben gave a light chuckle and kissed her on the cheek. The three of them would never again have a threesome together.

Even now, to this very day, that night will still get brought up in passing between Ben and Zach. When Ben wakes up in the morning and has the urge to masturbate it is always this night that he usually comes back to, always cumming within a few minutes. It is a memory free of habituation because it is a memory of something that will never happen again.

Bethany

I'm pretty sure I was the first girl that Ben had ever dated, at least in a semi-serious manner. I was 13 and he was 14 going on 15 that year. We met at his sister's birthday party sleepover. Well, that wasn't the first time we met, but it was the first time I guess I noticed him.

I remember he kept trying to sneak downstairs to "hang out," with all us girls and his dad kept coming downstairs to make him go back up to his room. The first time or two it was good for a nice laugh, as he was obviously trying to flirt with everyone, but after the 3rd and 4th times, you could tell that his dad was getting pretty angry.

The next day when everyone was waiting to get picked up, I had to stick around later since my mom was a late sleeper. I knew if she got there before noon it was going to be a miracle. The nice part of that, though, was that I got some time to hang out with Ben just watching old episodes of *Legends of the Hidden Temple* on TV.

Despite his over-the-top goofy approach to humor when he was around a crowd, at least at that point in his life, he was actually a pretty quiet boy. I remember finding it pretty charming the way we could just sit, exchange a few words and then watch TV. My house always had a lot of noise and yelling in it so this quiet time was refreshing.

Before I left that day, he very awkwardly asked me for my number, which back then just meant actually giving a house phone number. I agreed to it and a few days later he gave me a call.

We talked for about an hour and then we both agreed it was time to refocus our energy back to finishing homework. Within a few weekends we were hanging out back over his house. I felt bad because I wanted to try to show that I didn't want to hang out with his sister but at the same time I just wanted to be with him.

The first few "dates," if you can call it that I was really trying to divide my time evenly between the two of them, but as things developed my focus turned to just Ben.

He was sweet, he didn't pressure me into anything and again his house was always so quiet. This wasn't meant to last for very long though. I mean at that age what really does? We were both so young, but looking back there were signs that maybe things could have progressed more in time.

The turning point seemed to be at the times when we would be around my family. He never really wanted to interact with any of them. When we did, he was even more quiet than usual and always wanted to get me some where alone with him. It wasn't to do anything sexual; it was just like he wanted to get me back all to himself. As if he might have been jealous of others taking my time away.

The worst case of this was when we went out on my uncle's boat in the early summer. As soon as we went under the deck of the boat and laid down together, he didn't want to leave. Even after we threw down an anchor and everyone was swimming. He just wanted to stay on that little cot cuddled up with me, not interacting with anyone else.

I'll never forget how his face was pressed up against the back of my neck, his voice muffled from talking through my skin.

"Let's go out there."

"No, just stay and cuddle."

"Ben, we can do that anytime. I want to swim."

"But I want to be here with you."

"You'll be out there with me."

"It's not the same."

Then he would squeeze me tighter and we would lay for another twenty minutes, only to repeat the same process. Finally, I pushed myself away and went out to join everyone else. About five minutes later, Ben came out and got in the water, too.

He half-heartedly talked with my cousins, played a little catch with them, and again was ready to just go home. He seemed so distant and brooding. For someone who was only 14 it seemed too dark, even then. I just got that feeling like he was never really happy.

It was on his birthday, though, that he acted the most out of character and I'll never understand why. I remember I called him early on and wished a happy birthday. I forget why but we couldn't actually see each other in person that day. I still got him a gift though.

Around lunchtime though he called me to break up with me. I was completely caught off guard and he really didn't provide a reason for it. So naturally, as a young teenage girl I just wanted to get an explanation. I called his house and he didn't answer, but when he would, I remember hearing other people with him and I could hear him laughing with them.

I felt like the butt of some strange joke and it made me so mad. This was not the Ben I knew at all. I guess maybe he was put up to it or just had this big stroke of ego being around his new found friends that were his same age. I just know I was upset and I was being very vocal about that, but he just didn't seem to care.

I never would get a proper explanation for why he did that. Even a few years later, when we had hung out again, he just kind of shrugged it off as being a dumb teenage boy. It was rude, and I should have really stood my ground better to explain how not okay that was.

Many years after that, when Ben was dating around, we hung out and had sex. It was weird because it was the first time we ever had sex and going from dating so young to then very few interactions to finally sex seemed like a strange lifelong progression.

The sex was honestly just terrible. I think I was giving him too many sensations to take in at once (I'm a giver) and he finished within a few minutes of us starting. He was clearly embarrassed by his lack of stamina and I remember he was hinting at wanting me to leave pretty bad. I left him to process it all.

The last interaction we had was a few weeks later when he was trying to arrange a three way between me and another girl who lived nearby. We were both ok with making a go at it but just when I was telling Ben I was ready to come over he went completely silent. The next day he apologized and that was pretty much it for actually seeing one another in person.

    We still talk every now and again, but nothing really past the whole 'how are you' kind of conversation. I don't think I miss him but I do often worry about him being okay. I still see that teenage boy looking off into the distance, away from people and out in the water. He was floating along, just looking around at nature, but even there he wasn't at peace. He was in his head and all I wanted to do was help me to get out of it…but he never let me or anyone ever really try…did he?

Climax

It was dark and I had no sense of direction or purpose in the place in which I was standing. All of a sudden, a spotlight blasted through, illuminating myself and a small area around me. It was as if I was standing on a stage but I could hear nothing outside of the low hum of electricity that was emanating from this light source.

From the shadows emerged four men, one at each corner from where I was standing. They began to slowly walk inward, closer toward me, in unison as if they were controlled by the same silent hive mind. The faces had no definition, but they all reminded me of various men I had met over the course of my life. I could feel each of their traits surrounding me just as much as they were doing so physically. I was stuck.

I lowered myself down into something of a fetal position, -but I stayed on my feet. The men now towering over me, I was helpless to their whims. They just stood, saying nothing, not even looking at me. They just stood each looking across at each other. Nothing but that hum buzzing, breaking the pure silence. I looked up at that light, hoping it would blind me and help me to not see what might come next.

Suddenly one of the men grabbed me by the hair. I started to breathe heavier. A clump of my hair was held tightly in his hand. Then, the other three men moved in next to him, standing shoulder to shoulder. They all turned around and, in doing so, my hair twisted in the man's hand. I was forced to contort my head to alleviate the pain.

They began to walk, and I watched my hair become quickly taut in his hands, he was dragging me. All the while, the spotlight was following me and me alone. The men were hidden in shadow, only occasionally being touched by the light spilling bouncing off the dark surface that was underneath me. I tried to stand, but when I did the strong force of the man's grip pulled me down to the ground. He did not want me to stand, he wanted to drag me.

The distant sound of a car starting took over the buzzing noise. I could hear car doors opening and closing. I tried to look past the legs of the man dragging me but the pain was too unbearable, all I could focus on was trying to fight through it.

Then the man stopped. He pulled up on my hair, forcing me to stand. Looking down at my body, I could see the blood starting to pull on my legs from the burns brought on from being dragged on the floor. The van was now in sight, and two doors at the back swung open. The man pushed me into the van.

When he pushed me, it was not as simple as myself just falling into the back of this van. It was as if I was pushed into the air, I was floating, having no control over my movements or where I would land. As if some preordained force was guiding me to exactly where I needed to go. As I was floating, I rotated up so as to have my back landing perfectly on the floor of the van, where I was looking directly to the ceiling.

When I landed, the four figures were hovering again over top of me. Like a group of savage hungry animals peeling the flesh off of a fresh kill, the men started tearing away at my clothes. With grinding nails, they did not care whether they were scratching my skin so long as with each new grab, another bit of my clothing was gone.

Then I was naked, bloodied, bruised, barely able to find a solid breath. I was frozen in a deep state of shock, but I could hear a countdown in my head 3…2…1. With that hit of 1, I started screaming at the top of my lungs. I was yelling out as loud as I could, feeling the piercing screams ringing in my own ears, my vocal cords feeling as if they could snap at any moment.

The men pulled out duct tape. They began trying to put the tape over my mouth. The first few pieces were too drenched in saliva to stick to me but after many tries, the tape began to take hold. As they found success the tape took hold not just over my mouth but around my head, forming a bond that no amount of screaming would penetrate through.

Two of the men grabbed each of my arms and pinned them to the ground, kneeling on each with all their body weight. The other two spread my legs apart, kneeling and pinning much in the same way. All I could do was look down to see what might happen to me, what might be coming for me. Out of the shadows there he was, it was Ben.

He started by kissing each of my ankles and side to side, leg to leg he worked his way upwards. I could not move; I could not fight. He took off his pants.

Then I woke up. I woke up to another email from Ben that he had sent early this morning. It had been a year since he kicked me out of his house and he was still contacting me. I had him blocked everywhere but through email, and he would still regularly send me messages. Messages that ranged from words of hope, anger, denial, you name it. I was exhausted by it and had my own relationship now.

If Ben hadn't kicked me out that night I probably would have stayed, though. I would have stayed as long as it took until I could move away with Tom, but Ben didn't know this.

I deleted the email and got out of bed. When I went to the bathroom, I slid down my underwear and noticed they were soaking wet.

The Neon Demon

The drive to DC was a mostly forgettable, albeit far too brisk, drive down for Ben. While the simple comfort of just listening to music on the road was so peaceful, it was always the destination that caused the most stress.

In Ben's life, he had been to a few events over the years that had a larger media presence. Nothing would compare to what he was stepping into tonight though.

As he pulled up to the DC Armory, traffic was bumper to bumper. Even with his media parking pass, he was told the entire lot was full. He ended up parking three blocks away on a residential street and walking to the venue.

Ben was anxious. He had his laminated press badge with him, it was an easy in, but even despite this the amount of people pouring into the venue was a lot to take in. Luckily, the amount of attendants outside were numerous. Without even having to say a word, one of them saw the badge.

"Media! You media?!"

"Yeah."

"Head down the path here to the downstairs entrance, just knock they'll let you in."

The man just as quickly went back to directing traffic before Ben could ask any questions. He went to the door and knocked. A large imposing man opened it, saying nothing. Ben walked past and into the venue. He was instantly hit with flashing lights, loud pulsating music, and a crowd of media vendors waiting their turn to get inside.

"Name. Who are you with?"

"Benjamin. I'm with Boxing Champs."

"What's in the bookbag?"

"Lenses, camera, microphone."

"Alright head in, you're at row five."

Ben went in, walking past more large men guarding various parts of the venue. It was large but dark, the lighting all seemed to be focused directly at the ring. Every corner of the space was filled by people walking in, taking their seats. Ben had no idea where to go, so when asked, he just kept saying row five until a woman walked him over to the area. He had assumed he would be in the stands amongst the many others who paid money to see the fight but instead he was sat in the media pit.

This area was full of journalists, photographers, bloggers, etc. They all seemed to have computers, cameras, camcorders, anything in order to keep track of the fights. Ben sat silently in a row almost completely by himself. Only about one hundred feet in front of him was the ring. His instructions were simple, merely spectate until the fight was over and then get footage of something, anything, of the press conference afterwards. That was it.

There were three fights scheduled that night. The first was a small fight between two local boxers that were just on the bill as a warm up. The media around Ben did not seem all that interested and it was indeed an underwhelming fight. They were both pretty inexperienced and after a few rounds of dancing around the ring, the fight was called.

The next match was when things quickly ramped up. This was the first fight of the night to be televised and, while not the main event, the first real professional boxing match Ben had ever seen. His only point of reference was the film *Raging Bull* before tonight. The fighters were Robert Easter Jr. and Algenis Mendez.

The two men entered the ring. Mendez had white and red shorts, Easter Jr. wore silver and purple. Easter had almost a hula skirt like beading running all off the shorts. They were both small in size, something akin to flyweight or bantamweight. As the bell rang, they both began to furiously attack one another. They both had strong stamina and exchanged blows quickly. From the very start though, Easter seemed to be the more skilled fighter of the two. He danced around the ring, leading the charge, wherein Mendez only seemed to be acting in defense of his own body.

After only four rounds of a possible ten Mendez collapsed and was unable to get up. Although he was able to crawl after dropping to the mat floor, the moment he collapsed was so violent the image stuck with Ben for a long time. It was one thing to watch it on the television, but seeing another person just go completely dark in person was not something to be celebrated. Of course the crowd went wild at this moment, but nothing about it sat right with Ben. What you won't see or didn't see on TV in this case was the time it took for the medics to get Mendez out of the ring. He was dazed and could barely stand, more than likely sustaining a pretty severe concussion. The lack of empathy not only from the crowd, but also the media who just sat in indifference, knowing that the sooner he was gone the sooner the main event could start was astounding.

Boxing was never meant to be a pretty sport, but this was a world Ben now felt even more alien in. The sheer masculinity raging from each corner of the room was palpable, and it was something that Ben did not enjoy one bit.

After a long break, the main event was set to begin. The two men set to fight were Adrien Broner and Ashley Theophane. Of course, all the pomp and circumstance surrounding the match was built up to a fever pitch to anyone who had been paying attention. In his job duties leading up to the event, Ben had already been to a press conference at a DC nightclub as well as the official weigh in at a DC boxing gymnasium.

Theophane had sparkling gold shorts, while Broner wore silver and purple. The showmanship of both men was on clear display. Anyone in the know that evening had clear faith in the sure victory of Broner. At the various lead up events Ben overheard people commenting on how much of a mismatch the two fighters were. Theophane was just a much smaller size than Broner and what would ensue that evening clearly demonstrated that.

A constant barrage of head and body blows would confound Theophane, who never seemed comfortable or in control of the fight. Ben was engaged by the two men combatting in the ring but it was clear to even him that this was a one-sided affair. From his outsider perspective, he wanted

Ashley to take the fight simply on the principal that Broner was kind of a jerk, always taking chances to trade words, and even showing up excruciatingly late to the events leading up to the night.

In the ninth round, after constant blows to the body, the match was called in a TKO. Theophane never fell that evening, but the ref called it after Broner had him against the ropes and was landing a brutal fury of hits. Adrien Broner won and now Ben's job was to begin. He had to film the post-match press conference for anyone he could.

As the media began packing up, Ben made his way with the crowd of journalists to Broner's locker room, where it quickly became chaotic. During the transition, Ben was approached by a guy named Hawk, who was around his same age.

"Who are you here for?"

"Boxing Champs."

"Oh. Never heard of them, I'm with Ring Night. You ever done a boxing match before?"

"They're smaller, and no I haven't. It's been interesting."

"Yeah, well, now the fun begins."

Hawk ran through the crowd, getting as close as he could, much closer than Ben, who gave in to the pushing rather quickly. Having the bookbag didn't help matters much, either. After waiting for fifteen minutes, a part of Broner's entourage came out to the media.

"Broner will not be making any comments tonight, please leave. I repeat Adrienne Broner will not be making any comments tonight, so please move on."

The media present was not having it. Many in the crowd started yelling out, calling for Broner to speak. It even started to get heated, with the entourage member cursing back at the media. It seemed a lost cause. Ben walked back into the lobby where he ran into Hawk again.

"Not happening tonight?"

"Doesn't seem like it but you never know. You from around the area?"

"Yeah, well sort of, I'm in Baltimore."

"Cool, I'm here in DC. You got a card?"

Ben handed him a card, and Hawk handed Ben his in return. After a few more minutes of chatting about video equipment Ben, decided he was going to call it a night. As he walked to his car; in a not so friendly part of DC, even the cops who were around the Armory mentioned about being careful in that neighborhood. There was good reason to mug the folks who had enough money to spend on a big-time boxing match. Despite passing a few shady-looking characters, Ben made it to the car safely and took the long drive back home.

As he drove, he thought over how he would explain the situation to the owner of the company who hired him. He legitimately waited and waited to no results. It was the main goal of the night, though, and with the world of journalism this seemed to be the greatest sin. Of course, the email exchange was not a friendly one and through three days of work Ben was unsure if he was going to be paid at all. That is, three days of commuting from home to DC and the parking costs from each event.

Just when things seemed lost Hawk emailed Ben close to midnight saying that Broner finally emerged addressing the crowd almost an hour after he had left. He had offered Ben the footage but had to naturally wait until he could get it to his boss first, as in the boxing world the focus was on speed, and who could break a story the quickest. Once Ben had the file, he immediately sent it over to the owner.

After a few days passed, Ben finally got the notification of money transferred to his Paypal account. All of that time, energy, and effort amounted to $750 of untaxed income. After taxes, of course, even less.

The time spent on the project may have been something Ben had never seen before but he realized that it was not something he would have wanted to do daily. The feeling must have been mutual, because he never worked with Boxing Champs again.

Paprika

Shoes and shorts littered the locker room floor as the boys all changed clothes following gym class. The first bell started to ring, and Ben had to get through to Latin Class as fast as he could. It was only the sophomore year of high school, but with a connected middle school Ben had technically been going to Sparrows Point since 6th grade. This building was old hat.

Out of all the classes he had that year, Latin was the one Ben struggled with the most. It was just something that didn't make much sense, then again, all foreign language was tough for Ben. It was a normal, temperate day just as any other, the sun soaked into the classroom and Ben sat behind an old flirt of his, Missy. Missy was a close friend of Ben's younger sister Kara; she was a homely girl, a bit chunky but had a good libido. It was easy and at a time where Ben was a chunky hormonal teenager himself, it was the perfect fit.

The two had never had sex but made out a few times, and Ben would often try to find ways to get her up to his room while she "studied," with Kara. The moments would pass fast, but they were always good for a few seconds of libido-driven bliss. Ben would almost always masturbate immediately after to break his own internal tension. On one occasion in particular, Ben found himself so worked up that he spent the entire time kissing Missy's foot as she and Kara sat at the kitchen table, working away. Kara was unaware of what was going on and Missy was happy to oblige, making sure to raise her foot to Ben's face. It was a fetish that never matured into anything, but on that day her feet just felt like the most majestic thing in the world.

After a few minutes of class, the phone began to ring. Mr. Willems stepped away to answer it.

"Ok, yeah, I'll send him right up...Benjamin, the assistant principal would like to see you."

This was completely foreign to Ben. He had never been called to see the assistant principal before. There was one time but that was when he was being ferociously bullied way back in middle school. It was not on Ben's terms or behest, so this was a shock. Of course, as he stood up the whole class looked on, watching his every move, whispering amongst themselves as Ben walked out of the back door of the classroom.

As he took every little step closer to the main office, a sense of utter dread washed over Ben. He had no idea what could be going on, or what crime he could have committed. He checked in with the secretary and sat down at the small group of chairs that formed a waiting area. The office was always so brightly lit, in complete contrast of the dark reasons a student might visit, whether that be to talk with the guidance counselor or receive a reprimand from one of the three principals that formed the makeshift governing body of the school.

He was told to head back to the office and had to get directions from the secretary, as this was the one alcove of Sparrows Point, he did not fully understand. When he opened the door, he came upon the worst-case scenario. Not only was the assistant principal, Mr. Boblitz sitting at his desk but in a chair next to his was the school police officer, Mr. Ryan.

"Have a seat, Benjamin. Just give me one second." Mr. Boblitz was typing away at his keyboard as Mr. Ryan just looked at Ben, not saying a word. Ben could only fiddle his fingers, waiting, knee shaking, for what was going to come. Mr. Boblitz took a long sigh.

"Ok Benjamin, so I'm sure you're wondering why you're here."

"Yeah…"

"Well, it has come to our attention that a student has brought up allegations of sexual harassment against you. Now, what we are doing here is just trying to piece together the narrative. Of course, we take this very seriously, and we just want to get your side of the story. The best thing you can do now is be honest. Ok?"

"Yeah, sure. Uh do my parents know I'm here?"

"Yes, we called to let them know."

"Okay…"

"Now look, as much as we wish we could be anonymous about this, we can't really get to the bottom of anything unless you know who we are talking about. So, what we want to know is the extent of your relationship to Missy. We already sat down with her and your sister, so now we need to start with your version of everything."

"Well, what did they say?" Ben began to take quick breaks to quickly look out the window to try to give himself even a millisecond of escape from this small office. His nerves were shot and although he wasn't sure where this was coming from, he wished he could just fly out of the window away from it all.

"Look, Missy is claiming that you have been grabbing her butt during Mr. Willems class. Now I know Mr. Willems runs a tight ship, and I know you are a good student, so I am as baffled as you are, however we just need the full story."

"Where should I start?" It was as if Ben knew everything but it all appeared as a fragmented timeline. All he could remember was how it got to this point. At the core of it all was the fact that Ben did not want to date Missy, she was mad, she felt they connected and for Ben it was just fun. He didn't want to date, he never wanted to date but she did. This move, in Ben's eyes, was an act of respite.

"Wherever you'd like to."

"Well, I mean Missy is friends with my sister as you know, and we've been together I guess romantically a few times."

"Romantically how?"

"Well, you know, kissing, holding hands, making out…"

"So, no sex, then?"

"No, nothing like that."

"I mean we just would quickly meet up when my parents weren't home or…"

"Are your parents often not home when you are?"

"No, they are home a lot, just some days immediately after school that's all."

"Ok, because some things are already starting to not add up for me and Mr. Ryan here."

"How?"

"Well, it just seems as if you were viewing these interactions as more playful, Missy seemed to liken them to being more romantic in nature."

"I guess they could be, it just felt like fun to me."

"Well, it isn't fun to go messing with someone's emotions, now, is it? Would you want someone to do that to you?"

"No."

"Exactly."

The questions kept coming, as Ben would spend the next forty-five minutes in the office. Even through a change of classes, he was kept describing as many details about the affair as he could. Ben sat sweating in that chair, wondering why at the very least hadn't his parents tried to come to the school. He wanted them to at least be there as some sort of shield from all of this. Talking about intimate sensual details with someone was just overwhelming in so many ways.

"Well now, let's get to the heart of all this and I need you to answer me completely truthfully, okay?"

"Okay."

"Now did you touch Missy's butt, or have you been harassing her in class?"

"No."

"And you are sure of this?"

"Yes, I didn't."

"Okay, well, me and Mr. Ryan have to sort through everything, but for now you can go back to class."

"Am I in trouble? What now?"

"Well, we can't answer that yet, for now just head back to class."

Ben walked out of the office, note in hand. At this point, it was time for AP Social Studies and of course there was a pop quiz. Ben looked at the paper as if it was written in gibberish. He had no answers as to whether he was going to be suspended, expelled, have charges placed against him. It was a completely alien feeling. One wherein he could not even eat for the rest of the day. Everything seemed to float by him, all he wanted to do was get home to confront his parents, his own sister, as to why they weren't there for him in that office.

When he arrived home that day, Ben was in a complete fury. He instantly stormed up the steps to Kara's room. As he did, he could hear her room door slam shut and lock.

"What the fuck did you tell them?! What the fuck did you say, you fucking piece of shit! Why would you do that to your own fucking brother!" The yelling continued on and on. Ben felt bitterly betrayed that his own sister would paint a negative picture about him. He knew if she had said anything positive, he wouldn't have been interrogated in the first place. After a few minutes of banging, Ben gave up. He would have to wait another hour before his father would arrive home.

Today, somehow, was a different day and it was actually his mother who came home first. As he heard the car pull in the garage, he ran downstairs to meet her as she walked in the door.

"Did the school call you today?"

"No, what happened?"

"They didn't call you at all, or leave any messages?"

"No, what's going on?"

"Mr. Boblitz, you know the assistant principal."

"Yeah."

"Well, he and Mr. Ryan, the school officer interrogated me for an hour today about Missy."

"What'd you do?"

"I didn't do anything, and that's the problem, of course Kara painted a terrible picture of me, she sided with Missy."

"Well, what's going on now?"

"I don't know, they didn't give me an answer, I just went to class."

Ben's mother was livid, she really didn't get any notification from the school about anything. As Ben's father arrived home, he said that he too hadn't gotten a call or a message as well. Ben's mother left a message for the school asking for an explanation, as well as sending an email.

By the end of the week Ben, his mother, and father were all seen by the principal of the school. It was a complete overstepping of boundaries by the school, for which the principal was completely apologetic. Everything was completely dropped and the matter was never to be discussed again. Despite the anger that was felt from the whole family, they put it behind them.

The sad thing of it all was that there was a single day where Ben really did touch Missy's butt as they departed class.

Of course, in her story about it all it was blown up to a repetitive offense. For Ben's part, after he did it, he felt instantly dirty that something in his mind even suggested to commit such an act. Although Missy would look back and give him a chuckling smile, he knew it was wrong. The fact remained, though, that he did still do it.

Missy

I was with Ben for two years. We met on Match.com, a dating app for those who were more serious about finding a long-term relationship. I worked a long time as a flight attendant and had a lot of times in my life filled with partying and drugs. I was ready to let go of all that and begin to find the person I was going to be with.

When we matched, I was honestly drunk. I took one look over his profile and he looked like nothing more than a total tool. My whole purpose for even starting any conversation with him was to just troll him.

I think he didn't understand what I was trying to do or maybe he just wasn't paying enough attention but somehow the conversation moved past all of that. Next thing I knew I was meeting him for a drink in Towson.

Ben was a true curiosity to me. I remember that terrible outfit he wore onto our first date. He had red Vans, bright red jorts and a button up white tee with pizza slices all over it. It truly took all of my strength not to just laugh him out of the room. I figured I'd at least get a free drink out of the whole affair.

I wouldn't say he passed the first date test with flying colors; it was a bit awkward, but it was enough for us to go see a movie that night. We held hands and he semi-tricked me into going to a concert with him the following week.

He was cute, you know, and being around him was infectious. There was this innocent charm that he carried about that made it easy to want to spend more time with. However, the problem was that this could only go on for so long.

Ben had this serious issue with just overthinking. He was always so worried about things like money and didn't have any stability in what he did for a living. I also always felt like he held my bipolar against me. Like he told me in conversations when it came to kids especially that he didn't want to do that out of a fear of having a child with issues of any kind.

He was just too wishy washy and couldn't make a concrete decision with confidence on just about anything. I knew what I wanted in my life and that involved going back to school, but he felt like he had to stay in the exact spot he was at in order to keep things moving. It was this safety mindset that keeps a person from failing, but it also keeps them from gaining a true reward in life.

Looking back, I feel kind of sad for Ben in that regard. I tried so very hard to make sure he could overcome his issues, there just wasn't a return for me with the same level of care.

He proposed to me, we were set to get married in California. I was genuinely happy and I know my parents at least were excited, they liked Ben despite their reservations for our joint life decisions. It was a simple issue of commitment on every level. He just couldn't do it. There was an opportunity for a steady job, us being married, and a nice apartment in Atlanta in addition to a home back in Maryland that we could have rented out.

It was all something that could have been, a thought that has faded, at least for me. I still hope that he is doing okay, though, despite everything that happened between us.

What Dreams May Come

The hot summer sun could be felt immediately that July day in 1998, but Ben was eager with anticipation for his 8th birthday party. He slept in as he did almost every Saturday of his youth, but once he was up his excitement was palpable.

As a child, Ben and his family didn't get out much and when the backyard hosted only himself and his sister, it always felt sort of sad. So, to see it clamor with chatter and life was a refreshing change of pace.

The family guests began to trickle in, little by little. Ben's extended family was very large with many aunts, uncles, and a veritable cornucopia of cousins, all mostly around the same age. It was like having a schoolyard's worth of children all in one place.

While naturally a little shy, Ben still very much enjoyed being at the center of everyone's attention and affection. As family members wished him a happy birthday and gave him gifts or cards, it soon became overwhelming in the best way possible.

Little did Ben realize that this was to be the peak of all the birthday experiences he would ever enjoy. It was close to the last time that the entire family would be together, and things would seem as innocent as they would ever be.

Ben's father was at the grill, preparing burgers and hot dogs for everyone while so many cousins ran around the back yard. They all gathered around either the pool or the light blue swing set that had two swings and another seated swing that about 4 small children could sit in at once while a parent pushed along. If you climbed along the set, your hands would always smear with the fading blue paint from it.

The pool hosted most of the older cousins. Ben's father was building a deck to walk out from the second floor of the house. It was nothing grand in scale, just something that you could walk out on to see the whole yard from below. While he had locked the door leading out to it, a few of the more resourceful cousins managed to get it open and were taking turns jumping from it into the pool. This was something Ben immediately wanted to try, but his father forbid it, getting openly mad about the whole situation. Sure, maybe someone could have gotten hurt but it was all in the spirit of having fun.

After all the uncles, aunts, and grandparents had finished eating it was time for big moment, the cake. Each year, there were two cakes made. One was vanilla and the other was chocolate so whatever your preference, you would not be left behind. One was a Ninja Turtle head with the proper blue icing on the bandana for Leonardo, Ben's favorite. The other was a Pikachu, looking a little off brand but for being made without a mold was still impressive.

After the eponymous happy birthday song was sung, Ben triumphantly blew out his candles. Whatever the wish was has been forever, lost to time, but it is not hard to imagine that it might have been for every day to be like this one.

As he began opening up his presents Ben was ecstatic at his tidings this year. Not only did he receive a few much-sought-after Beanie Babie's, but he also made a cool fifty dollars. At this point he could retire and just live off that money for the rest of life, or until he wanted to buy a few new games for his Gameboy.

After presents, the familial guests all began to slowly leave the party. They took some pizza slices, a little bit of cake, and said their final happy birthdays to Ben. This was the sad and lonely part that Ben never wanted to see happen.

As the air became more and more quiet, the realization that every day was not to be like this started to sink in. Ben tried in vain to get Tony, his closest cousin to stay the night, as someone that he could talk to about the day and live in the afterglow with just a bit longer. Given his medical condition with cystic fibrosis though, this was just not a possibility.

The party, the dream, it was over for Ben and he would swing on the swing set that once had a child in every seat. Looking to his left and to his right, reimagining everyone who was there earlier. He let the ghosts dance around in his head for just a bit longer.

The sun was setting and the mosquitos were coming out. It was time to go inside. As his parents prepared for bed, Ben sat in the living room on the tufted blue couch, looking up at the banner that read "Happy Birthday". It would be gone tomorrow, but for now he just stared up at it.

It began to lose meaning as Ben was drifting to sleep, but for one final moment he remembered how, in that early morning stupor of coming down the stairs, his heart began to race for deep down he knew for a little while this house would be filled with a lifeforce that was rarely repeated.

Dreams never came that night but they didn't need to because Ben lived a true dream that day, one that would never be repeated again.

Perfect Blue

The desk, the desk was wrong, it was the one with the cubby that you could shove papers into. It was pointless, as all Ben wanted to do was sit and let his leg shake up and down. It helped with the anxiety, it quieted things down, but not this type of desk. If Ben were to attempt a single motion of his leg, it would quickly ricochet off the cold metal and pop the desk upwards, causing a noticeable commotion.

It was just one more thing on the long list of all the reasons why this day was feeling like the worst day of Ben's life to that point. The day was nowhere near being complete either.

The substitute teacher that day was Miss Dotty, she carried with her a terrible lisp on top of an unusually loud voice and the students could never take her seriously. As they snickered, she would start to quickly yell at the classroom.

"Quiet down class…quiet down!" She would drone on as she scribbled equations on the chalkboard. It was a low drool of a voice, mixed with a large nasal inflection. Harsh on the eardrums, no matter what the level.

She would be no help during any of the math problems, either. Ben was already struggling and every time he would go up to her desk to check on his answers, he was told which ones were wrong. If he asked though, all that Miss Dotty could do was to reference her answer sheet. She didn't even know what math was involved, so she was no help.

The frustration grew even greater. Ben was feeling defeated. He just wanted the day to be over. Then Harold, sitting directly behind Ben, started flicking at his ear. The act of having one's ear jabbed at is something that does not come without an outward response, much in the same way that hitting your nose will produce tears.

After a few quieter attempts at masking the cries of pain that came with each flick Ben had had enough of it. He turned around and lashed out at Harold.

"Stop flicking my ear!" Ben yelled now facing Harold.

"Ben! What is going on?" Miss Dotty shouted almost immediately.

As Ben tried to explain the situation, Miss Doty retorted that she did not see anything and if he had another outburst he would be sent to the principal's office. This is a sentence on par with death in the second grade.

Ben was mad, he knew that if the regular teacher was here, this wouldn't be happening. He knew he could get his regular desk back and could have someone to properly help with his classwork. It was all too much and this day just had to end.

In a flash, Ben asked to go to the bathroom. Some kind of escape was necessary. Despite Miss Dotty being apprehensive, he lied and said it was an emergency. She let him leave the class and go about his business.

While it wasn't a complete emergency, Ben still did have to use the restroom. For a few fleeting moments it seemed like this might be the remedy to change the fortunes of the day. This was the reset button for everything. However, it was not to be. While in the bathroom sitting in the stall, an older boy kicked the door open in his stall, smacking into Ben's legs.

The door was a thin metal, and it knocked his knees against one another and the boy ran away just as quickly as he committed the action, laughing the entire time. It was an invasion of privacy and a moment that Ben would never forget. For the rest of his life, he would always check the locks of the stalls and feel a little nervous when he would see a pair of shoes walking by his stall.

For the time being, though, this was the final escalation of the day. There was no going back and Ben needed to escape. As he paced around the bathroom, he remembered a pair of doors that were nearby. A few weeks prior, as he was going to gym class, he realized the doors did not have an alarm on them. They were just bare doors to the freedom of the outside world.

He knew about alarms on doorway exits after accidently going through a pair at a Burger King the summer before. He tripped the alarm, sending the entire restaurant into an uproar. He was so embarrassed that day; he wailed crying the whole way home, saying he was sorry. This was an easy fix by the staff, but he knew that everyone was staring at the silly boy who triggered the alarm, it was just too much at the time.

With his knowledge set, he knew that these doors would not trigger any such notifications and so, being done with the day, he walked right through. It was a still, warm fall day with plenty of lush colors upon the trees. His parents' home was a town away, but his grandmother's home was in walking distance from the school. In the many summers he spent there with his cousins, they would often walk as a group to the school to play at the playground so the path to get there was very clear in Ben's mind.

He simply walked away from the school, from that Hellish nightmare that brought never-ending pain on this day. He made sure to take the path that would get him away from the perimeter of the school the fastest so that no one would see him. It felt like some stealth action videogame before that would even become a genre.

So, he walked and in about twenty minutes, he was at his grandmother's house. Her car wasn't parked there and after knocking a few times with no answer he simply pulled at the handle. To his surprise the door was unlocked. With that he walked in and sat on the couch, petting her dog, just sitting in the silence.

After a few minutes he heard her car pull in the driveway and he had opened the door for her, as she had groceries in both arms. She stopped in her tracks as if she was seeing a ghost.

"Benjamin, what are you doing here?" she said with a cried expression.

Ben stayed silent, simply opening the door so she could walk in. Instead of letting out a flurry of emotions like he kept telling himself he would do, he said nothing. He couldn't put on some show for his grandmother, he wanted to, but just couldn't.

She sat down the groceries and called the school. After a heated exchange from the guidance counselor (who at first thought she picked Ben up without notifying anyone) she was able to explain that he walked to the house. She would, of course, bring him back right away.

In the short time since Ben left, the school had completely locked down and there were staff looking everywhere around the building for him. They were almost about to notify the authorities, but the call was made just before that happened.

Ben's grandmother than drove him back to the school where he was immediately ushered into the principal's office. To the credit of the principal, he just wanted to hear what had happened. Now was when Ben burst into his flurry of emotions. He went on about how bad the day was and how inept Miss Dotty was, it was all just too much so he ran away.

The principal understood but said how that was not right. *You can't just run away from your problems.*

As it was now almost the end of the school day, Ben was brought back into the classroom. However, the principal did not want him to sit in with the students to finish the day. Instead, he sat Ben down at one of the Macintosh computers where Ben would spend the last thirty minutes playing Number Munchers until the final bell rang.

When he got back to his grandmother's, he again sat in silence, waiting for his father to pick him up. His mother and father were of course upset but they later recognized that it was actually quite ingenious that Ben was able to put together so many elements to formulate an escape plan like that.

Within a week that door he used as he fled the school out of had an alarm trigger put on it. The only limitation that kept this from being put in place before was budgeting. After the incident though, the county all of a sudden found the money to make it happen.

Jackie

Ben was a fucking asshole. I'm sorry, there just isn't another way to put it. We went out on a few dates and there was seriously no point to any of it. I think we met on OkCupid and I thought he was looking for a relationship. It was strange from the beginning. I mean he seemed out of my league, but he always assured me it wasn't an issue. I don't know why I believed him at his word.

Our first date, he drove down to where I worked at Starbucks and picked me up. We went all the way back to his place and we were potentially going to go for a walk at a park nearby. Instead, we ended up sharing a shower and I was trying to have sex with him. I liked his body, but he didn't seem interested at all. He tried but after a few non-starting moments he confessed that he wasn't in the mood and we sort of just awkwardly finished up.

After that, we just talked for a bit in his living room talking about the emo bands we each enjoyed in our high school days. He eventually played drums on his game Rock Band and then drove me back home.

I figured that would be it, but a few weeks later he messaged me about hanging out again and so I suggested a bar that I liked near my place. We met for a few drinks and I must have had a few too many because I started getting bold in my questioning. I asked him about his motivation with me and why we weren't dating. I'm sure he was uncomfortable and I just didn't care. We almost had sex, then he disappeared and now he was back out of the blue for what? Was he bored? Was he just using me?

As we drank more, I can remember enough to know that he had to give me a ride home…well that is the part that he can go fuck himself over. We were arguing, like yelling arguing and then next thing I knew I was on the road stumbling home. He kicked me out of his car and left me on the side of some residential area that I had never been to before with a phone that was nearly dead. I'm lucky I got back home at all that night.

A few days went by and I sent him a long message of how horrible his actions were that night and I'll give him credit for at least replying with an apology but I mean fucking-A, who does that?

The last I ever saw from him was about a year or two later when he suddenly showed up on my suggested matches through OkCupid. I was in Arizona and felt like it was some ghost following me to a city far away from Baltimore. I swiped right on him just to see if he would let his curiosity get the best of him too.

He must not have felt the same way, as we didn't match.

The Circle

This room, this one room Ben must have walked into over a thousand times in his life. He knew it like every other inch of this house he practically grew up in. It was not the same room this night. It was something from a nightmare, and Missy lay in the center of it, shrouded in darkness. Ben attempted to bring some light into the space but Missy did not want it. The darkness of her mind needed the proper accompanying space.

Ben tried to at least offer a consoling hand to try to show Missy that he was there for her but she snapped at it as quickly as she noticed it moving toward her. He knew what was wrong, it was the other half of the extreme that consumed Missy's life. The highs were monumental but the lows were consumed by the type of dread that anyone who is not afflicted would never fully comprehend.

"Can I get you anything at least?"

"No, I'm fine, I just need to lay here for a while."

"Can I lay next to you, maybe?"

"No, just let me lay here, I just want to be alone."

Ben knew that there was no way to change what the brain chemistry had done. It was something that no words could ever really fix. They had talked about possibly trying hypnosis as a tactic, but it would never come to fruition. It was to be a long regret for Ben that he didn't try harder with this plan. That hypnosis was a fetish for him just made things more complicated and his own way of overthinking it all created a mental barrier for him to try.

Missy asked him to close the door as he was walking out of the room and he looked back, nodding. As he took that glance over to Missy though he saw past the frizzled façade that she carried. He saw a glint in her eye that spoke not of sweetness but of something crying out. An unspoken message for help that made him pause as the door was halfway shut. He stopped and pressed on further.

"Are you sure there isn't anything I can do?"

"I told you to go, now please just close the door and let me be."

"If I shut this door and you do something to hurt yourself, I couldn't live with that." Ben had remembered that for Christmas that year Missy bought him a straight razor kit. It came complete with individual razor blades and something internally connected those dots, that maybe it could have gone this far.

"Why would I do anything to myself...why would I..." Missy started fumbling around under her pillow. Ben wanted to lunge at her and grab the pillow away but worried that it might cause more harm than good. After a few moments, Missy had in her hand an unwrapped straight razor.

Ben reached out and she placed it in his hand. In a flash, he took it and threw it in the small green trashcan in the bathroom. Before Missy could do anything, he ran back into the room. She started crying.

"I'm sorry, I'm sorry. I swear I wasn't going to hurt myself. I promise I wasn't."

"Shh...it's ok, really I know. I believe you it's ok."

Missy was rocking back and forth, repeating her apology over and over again. Ben just kept holding her close and telling her not to worry. He had to get her out this darkness, out of this cave that seemed to only grow larger as the eyes were consumed by the lack of any light. That moment when you have just been staring at black so long the room fades into a mass of endless shadow.

"Let's go lay down in bed, our bed." Missy just stayed sitting, rocking, crying.

Ben was trying to get her to her feet. At a mere one hundred and twenty pounds, Ben actually weighed a touch less than Missy and he didn't have the strength to carry her completely. She would have to help get herself up. It was no use though, as with each attempt to get her up things only became worse.

Ben would try and lift her and she skulked back down to the ground, each time the crying turning more into wailing. The words were just screeches and creaks as the muscles of the throat broke down. Missy was becoming angry, the mind rising out of the dread and into a place of hatred. Ben, in her mind, had turned from some kind of tender figure to the cause of the pain.

"If we weren't here, stuck here it would be different." Missy began to mutter with a low drawl as she sat with her head on her legs.

Ben could barely make out what she was saying and he asked her to repeat what the words were. Missy slowly lifted her head up and opened her eyes that dripped a gush of water from each one, like that of a plastic cup as you slowly squeeze it in the hand. Ben stared down at her and tried again to get her off the ground.

That was the tipping point for Missy who sprang up and began to rush around the house. The first place was the closet where she grabbed a few pieces of her clothing. Then to the bathroom to grab deodorant, her toothbrush, and hairbrush.

Ben was following swiftly behind trying to get her to stop. What had begun as simple swats in the air turned to full slaps from Missy as Ben attempted to hinder her progress.

"Missy stop, Jesus fucking Christ, cut it out. Where do you think you are going to go?"

"Home, I'm going home for a little while, I just need to go."

"Georgia? You're going to drive all the way to Georgia tonight. It's almost fucking midnight."

The packing did not stop and the interactions were growing more violent. Missy had warned Ben of something like this happening. She had told him to never let her leave if she did and he finally had to make sure it wasn't going to happen. After she put on her shoes and was about to get her bookbag filled with everything for the road he stopped Missy for a moment. He looked her in the eyes and gave her a hug.

Missy did nothing at first but leave her arms by her side. She caved in though after a few seconds and gave him a hug in return.

"Ok, but I still just have to go."

Ben did not let go though. Missy started pushing away but Ben was not letting go.

"You told me not to let you go out that door, and you aren't going to get that far."

Missy struggled and started using her extra weight to her advantage. After a bit of pushing and shoving, they ricocheted off of the wall, forcing Ben to lose his balance. He hit his head pretty hard and was now on the ground. He was still conscious, but as if they both shared in the trauma to the brain something just snapped back in place for Missy.

Her voice, demeanor, even appearance all seemed to change in the same way an animal content after a hunt looks. It is just docile and tender. Missy helped Ben to his feet, and this time wrapped her arms around him.

"Thank you." She whispered to him, as tears began to form again.

"It's okay, let's just go to bed."

The bed was covered in misplaced items that Missy had thrown about in her quest to pack as quickly as possible. The night had proven to be a marathon, and they each took a side of the bed to clean it off. Weakened by the night, they didn't say anymore words, just shuffled along, completely drained.

They each climbed under the sheets and held each other close. Ben passed out within minutes of his head touching the pillow. Missy looked up at the ceiling for a little while after Ben was asleep, she could tell by the last twitch his arm made each night when he drifted away. She could see the darkness was all around her and the dread was just as quickly setting back in.

On one side she knew that Ben was asleep and she could easily go get another razor from the bathroom. On the other she also still had this anxiety to run away. The only redemption was closing her eyes. Maybe if she fell asleep fast enough, the thoughts would be quieted and that by morning it would all be ok.

Missy looked over to Ben with envy, for she knew there wasn't some chemical imbalance controlling him at every turn. She envied Ben for his simplicity and would never tell him that it was triggered by an overdraft notice from his bank. She knew she had no control in this relationship, she was at the mercy of every decision Ben made, good or bad.

Knock Knock

It was a hot July day when Ben and Zach started playing basketball. They met at the court of the elementary school Ben attended long ago. As they drove up to meet one another, they both had their stereos blasting. Zach filled the air with hip hop beats from the mid-2000s, while Ben was letting his car pelt out modern electronic goodness.

They played one on one in a game called fifty and with each round the stakes became more serious. A typical session would involve six to seven games back-to-back, and today was no different. Zach and Ben were evenly matched, although neither was any kind of phenom at the sport. Today Zach would take the *crown* by four games to three.

On a good day, the games would be interspersed with musings about each other lives. It was a chance to catch up and also release some pent-up energy. For Zach, it always seemed to be much higher stakes than for Ben. He just enjoyed playing and, since they had been meeting regularly to do so since the high school days, it was always a place of nostalgia.

Ben was busy commenting on another girl he had met online. This time another one from Craigslist. Zach for his part always listened and never challenged Ben's way of going about life. In fact, there may have been a little bit of envy in the air. Zach was in the middle of his own tumultuous relationship, one of many that he would go through in his life. It was always quite interesting looking at these two through a microscope. As it would be that Zach, over his life, would find himself wrapped up in more committed relationships, but the results were always the same. A few months would pass, and then it would be all over.

In spite of this, Zach would never let his thoughts on any relationship go more than surface level. If asked directly he would just say things were going okay or good, to get anything more would require asking the same questions a few times over. Ben, though, was an open book, maybe to a fault.

He would love, especially at this stage of his life, to comment on his many romantic conquests. In his mind, that is exactly what these were, conquests or stories to tell. Maybe he didn't really like himself after reflecting on his manipulative actions? On the basketball court though, he was the man.

"So, look, I met this chick on Craigslist, I just put up an ad saying like 'hey I'm into hypnosis, if you're into it just hit me up'."

"So, she hit you up and how do you know she ain't gonna kill you?"

"I mean I don't but like we've been talking for a few days now. She's a bit older than us but like she's down in DC, apparently working for some government peeps."

"Damn man that's dope."

The talking was always different between the two of them when they played. Lily had pointed that out to Ben a few years earlier when they were still together. She told him how he just acted and even sounded different around Zach. It was the first inkling of what Ben would think of as this chameleon skin he could wear around others. Much like the lizard though, the reflection of this trait always made him feel slimy and underhanded. It was old habit by now and the sun was setting.

As the last game ended with a close victory by Zach, the two decided to head to their favorite after-basketball destination, Red Brick Station. It was a tavern that was about thirty minutes away from where they lived. It was always like that with this small town, everything entertainment-wise always seemed to be a thirty-minute drive away in any direction.

They parked among the strange amalgamation of age groups. Children with their parents enjoying the outdoor air as they shopped for clothes. Couples going to the movies to have a nice weekday date. Future lovers awkwardly meeting for the first time, barely able to summon the strength to say a first name out loud, for fear of it being the wrong person.

Then there were those like Zach and Ben who were just going to get drinks, blowing off steam and reminiscing about moments long passed by.

"Remember when you won class president our senior year?" Zach would mention to Ben.

"Yeah, you were supposed to be my full-time bodyguard, where were you in the hallways man?"

They would laugh as Zach ordered a beer and Ben ordered his typical watermelon crush. The sweet, sugar laced drink made for the perfect thirst quencher after playing so many rounds of basketball, even if it would leave the already parched Ben more dehydrated as the night wore on.

Unlike the very regimented eating habits of Ben, Zach would eat at different times, often skipping meals throughout the day.

"I haven't ate since breakfast," Zach would mention as they both looked through the menu. Ben, being a creature of habit, already knew what he was going to get before they even sat down. It was to be crab toast or essentially crab dip on toast. Ben already had dinner before they met up, knowing that he would possibly be eating one more thing before the day was out, he had made sure to keep it light. The caloric intake was always an important factor. Ever since the year he lost seventy pounds just from counting calories, the habit never truly dissipated.

Zach, on the other hand, was a menu explorer. He took his time considering many different factors, but almost always settled on a burger. That was the ultimate decision this evening, picking out the Red Brick Burger and starting out with an appetizer of nachos.

Even as they drank and watched whatever random sport was on the televisions around the bar, Ben could feel that bit of sweet saliva hitting his palette. That rush of endorphins to the brain that, when at the right level of hunger, made you smile with glee as you were awaiting food to come.

This was, in fact, one of the factors that contributed to Ben's weight problems in the first place. That sensation and joy would become so overwhelming over the otherwise grey moments of life, he would never want to stop eating. This would lead to many meals of utter indulgence, causing a calorie surplus each day. Combining this with a general lack of exercise caused many stints of weight gain after about age eleven or twelve, all the way through to Ben's early twenties.

They ate and drank plenty that night. Ben managed to get through three crushes and Zach had four beers. Ben, being so skinny now, it did not take much to get a buzz going. The unfortunate truth is that Ben was also the one who drove the two to the bar in the first place.

In the midst of it all, Ben began messaging the woman in DC, who herself was out with friends that night. Their connection had been through hypnosis but she still wanted to actually go on a date with Ben first before anything else. Ben would often push his luck to see if he could bypass this requirement, but to no avail. The only reason he didn't want to do it was only because of the travel time involved. At his immature stage of mentality, if Ben wasn't getting any sex out of the deal, he wasn't going to waste the gas to do it.

Tonight, was different though, and a little unexpected. With her own evening get-together, the drinks were flowing in DC as well. Whereas Ben was typically the flirty one of the conversation, the texts were getting more risqué as the night went on. Of course, all the while Ben was filling Zach in on all the juicy details.

They were both reveling in it and, although Ben was typically sparse on the gritty details of his life, he was always so eager to gloat to Zach, especially of his impending or previous escapades. It was as if it was the only relatable factor or connection he could share with Zach.

As they were about to leave, the waitress brought the check. Ben, feeling high on the hog, wrote down his phone number, a gesture that would never receive reciprocation from the woman serving them that evening.

With shaky knees and a boisterous disposition Ben and Zach left the bar. As Ben went to the restroom, he told the woman in DC that he could come over tonight. She actually agreed and Ben was elated.

The drive back home, with Ben dangerously behind the wheel, was filled with electronic tune goodness, that Ben belted the words out to. This was something Zach found so ridiculous he had to film and put it on Snapchat for all his followers to see.

Even in his drunken state, Ben still felt the need to freshen up before making the trek down. He stopped home, where his sister was staying with him at the time and hopped in the shower.

In the spaces in-between, he decided to push his luck even further with the woman, playing into her hypnotic kink. He had told her to stare into what she called her "hypnocube," and begin touching herself in anticipation of his arrival. He also stressed that when he got there she stay completely undressed, leaving the door unlocked so they could start fucking right away.

All of it she went along with, no questions asked. It was endless joy for Ben, who quickly got out of the shower and made his way to DC.

After asking for the address, he was instantly sent it and only a little over an hour drive stood between him and his prize.

The drive down was uneventful, as Ben had come out of his drunken buzz with the nice hot shower. DC was still an area that, even though Ben had been there plenty of times for video gigs and weddings over the years, still felt confusing at times. This was no more evident than when Ben mistakenly went down a one-way street, not realizing the mistake until a taxi cab driver was furiously blowing the horn.

Luckily, it was at the very start of the street so Ben was able to quickly course-correct, heading down the proper road, this was only possible though because of how late it was now. Just a little past midnight.

He parked and let her know he was there. She gave him the apartment number and he buzzed the front door. Within a split second he was let in, and went up the steps. His heart was fluttering. Now the real nerves were setting in. He knew the woman but only from a few scant pictures and short phone conversations. This could be a set up for him, as he goes in there could be someone ready to attack.

The hormones were raging though, and none of this mattered. As he approached the door it was unlocked as he'd instructed, and the entire apartment was pitch black. The only light was coming from a room just around the corner of what appeared to be an immediate dining room/kitchen set up. It was a flickering light show and Ben immediately followed it.

As he walked into the room, she was there staring into this cube of flashing lights, laying naked and sprawled out, masturbating with a low tone of sensual groans. She was truly in a trance as Ben approached her. He began peeling off his clothes as quickly as he could. As he did the groaning stayed consistent, like that of a record skipping after playing each song from a track list. It was so many fantasies for Ben rolled into one and his erection was throbbing as he finally took his boxers off.

The first reaction he had was to divert her trance away from the cube. Thinking quickly, he remembered from all the sensual hypnosis porn he had watched over the years there were many that had men using their dicks to entrance a woman. So, with that flash of inspiration, he tried it and the woman immediately took to it. Her gaze was so focused on Ben's cock that he almost came right then. He held it together though and she asked if she could start sucking it and after some light teasing to wait for his command she did so.

Ben always felt awkward with blowjobs and even though she was good at it, he quickly grew bored and pushed her head back so that he could penetrate her. The typical procedure for Ben was to not wear a condom for such an action. It was not like he didn't know about possible diseases or pregnancy, but he just enjoyed the sensation of each new partner too much to want to create a barrier for it all. Plus, with Lily he was so used to pulling out that it was second nature.

However, tonight the only option was the condom or else she was not going to have sex with him. After trying to talk her away from it, Ben caved in and put the condom on. Immediately the ecstasy took over. She was immersed now in

Ben's eyes and Ben was in hers. The eye contact during sex was always important for Ben, as it just created this trance for anyone he was having sex with. The best moment was when he could match the climax with his lover. While he would not come, he could feel her deep release, which was the greatest pleasure he would want to give.

They were at it for at least an hour until she mentioned feeling satisfied with everything. Ben was sore and tired too from a long day of sports, drinks, and driving.

As they laid next to one another in the afterglow of the evening, Ben put a set of dog tags on, probably intentionally, to create a draw to them from the woman. She asked about the meaning behind them and Ben mentioned Lily. That is who they were from, a gift that seemed silly many Christmases ago, but took on a new life after their breakup.

The woman was not impressed with Ben's talk of his deep love remaining still for Lily. She was ten years Ben's senior, so her jaded perspective was unlike what Ben was used to. He didn't enjoy her candor and took a slight offense to her questioning Ben's line of reasoning. It was a little too much criticism for Ben to take at the time and he soon found himself wanting to leave the apartment. She offered him a room for the night, but he used the tried-and-true excuse of needing to work early the next day.

As the next few days went on the conversation between the two became less and less frequent, until finally it ended. Ben would never see the woman again and even with a few more efforts posting to Craigslist a few years later, he would never get a response from her. The cycle of getting a short stint of satisfaction, followed by deep alienation, and then eventual regret played out as it did far too many times in Ben's mid-twenties.

Mary

On the first date, Ben took me to see the 34th street light show in Hampden. As we crossed the street, walking together, he offered to take my hand as a type of safety net. It was a way to hold my hand but the gesture was a sweet one.

It was my first time seeing the lights and while it was a little underwhelming for what I felt it was made out to be, it was still really fun.

A few days later he took me out to dinner at one of those places where it is a few restaurants all in one spot. Like a big lunchroom for adults. He suggested an arepa, which I'd never tried before. It didn't blow me away but I was glad I tried it.

That same night we went back to his place and made love for a few hours. I never ever climax without my toys which I didn't have that night so it ended up being a bit frustrating for me. However, at the time at least, I thought he'd finished inside me.

I was terrified but also far too timid to ask a guy I'd only been out with a few times if he came inside me. I just accepted it as a thing for some reason. I was scared and the next day I picked up the Plan B pill to try and protect myself. I had this internal fury toward Ben and he just kept trying to talk to me like nothing happened.

Finally, I confronted him about it in a message. He was shocked and swore that he did it for show in order to put a finite end on our evening together. Even now I'm not sure if he was lying about his orgasm or lying about the fact that he faked his orgasm and really did finish.

We had one more time of "hanging out" together after that, which was really just about sex for us both. I was still living with my ex-boyfriend and was kind of seeing someone else. I was playing really hard to get because I just wasn't all that interested and that seems to have some kind of magic in it.

The whole time we were fucking he just would repeat how much he loved me over and over again. He wanted me to say it back to him and I eventually lamented with the preface that I was merely saying it back, there was no true emotion behind it. He said that was good enough and we kept going.

We still talk today and he has the same pattern of small talk followed by telling me how we are going to get married one day. I think he just feels safe saying it to me because he knows how farfetched it is. Or maybe he doesn't. Either way, I know the times when I felt more strongly about him he was a stranger, but since I've been distant he has been trying much harder to try to see me.

    I kind of wish I could just say that this is the only way I can make sure you'll love me. I have to keep you distant because the second I give in an inch you'll probably disappear again. I just won't understand why he wants it to be this way. Maybe just a form of some kind of self-torture?

Us

Roxy was laying down when she heard the door close shut, right out front. In her instant reaction, she started barking. What Ben knew was just a welcome had for so many years sent people taking a more cautious approach to the house. The only difference this time was the limp in Roxy's step.

Before leaving to go to China with his sister, Ben was concerned about Roxy's nail. It looked discolored, and a limp was slowly starting to form. The day before they were set to leave, Ben had asked his parents to keep an eye on it, going to the vet if necessary. They had said they would let him know.

It had been a wonderful two-week vacation seeing the temples, malls, and old cities of China with his sister, but upon returning home, the first thing Ben wanted to see was Roxy. When he did, he saw that her step had become even worse. The first thing he did was schedule an appointment with the vet right away.

Money was tight, and the last thing Ben wanted to do was spend more after two weeks of not only spending but not working any more gigs. It was a worst-case scenario.

The vet looked at the foot and found an infection from the nail being impacted. They trimmed the nail further despite Roxy's cries of pain and gave medication to try to deal with everything. Roxy had dealt with infections before, but now at ten years of age it seemed that everything took much longer to deal with.

After about a week, things did not improve and the limp was getting worse. Roxy tried to push through the pain, tried to keep up with Ben, tried to chase the squirrels in the back yard. It was all in vain though, and the signs of improvement just were not happening.

It was time, the time to look up what steps to take in order to help to end this pain, the pain which just never seemed to heal. It took two days just to summon the strength to search for it online, and then he had to make the call.

"Hello this is Peaceful Passing, my name is Grace, how can I help you?"

"Hi…uh this is Ben I was just calling about…" Ben had tears starting to form. He had to pause or he knew from experience that he would start crying. The tremoring lip started slowly, but was building.

"Hi Ben, were you calling about your pet."

"Yes, her name is Roxy, she just hasn't been doing very well lately, and I think it might be time." The tremors were worse, the droplets of water started to flow down the cheek and a few steady drips were hitting his shorts.

"I'm so sorry to hear that Ben, you can take a minute if you need to, but we can schedule a time to come out, if you want to, today."

"Yes, we can, and everything happens that same day?"

"Yes, we can come at the end of the week, if you have time."

Ben looked through the calendar on his phone to make sure that everything worked out okay. It also gave him a moment to wipe up his tears and take a few deep breaths.

"That works here."

"Okay we will be there at 11a.m. on Thursday."

With that, the phone went silent and Ben looked out the window, crying, to which Roxy came walking in to the room to inspect what was wrong. In her typical gesture, she rubbed her nose on his leg. The limp was worse than ever, but she was still committed to checking in on Ben's wellbeing.

He sat himself down on the floor, taking the glasses off his face. She started licking Ben's face, even as the tears continued to flow. In her mind it was just yummy saltwater, but Ben knew exactly what he had done. He picked the day that would be Roxy's last on this Earth and she had no idea what was to come. There was nothing Ben could say either, that would change the situation, she had no concept of life or death or even the proper time. It was hopeless, but maybe it was for the better. Ben knew how many days he had left with Roxy so he wanted to make sure they would be good ones.

Ben went to the pet store and got all the favorite foods and treats Roxy had enjoyed over the years, spoiling her for the remaining days she had. It was a last gesture of goodwill against the pain that he knew she was in.

Then, before he knew it, the day was here. All that morning Ben was on a video call with his sister and her boyfriend, so they could see Roxy one more time from China. They were heartbroken and just wanted to absorb every minute they could, even virtually. The moments of tears were only broken up with comments of how much they were going to miss Roxy.

As the knock came and Roxy began barking, Ben had to hang up the phone. The technician greeted Roxy and, despite the continued barking, sat down on the couch to give her the attention she wanted. Ben shook the technician's hand and they went through the process together.

"There is no rush, whenever you are ready, we can go ahead and get things started. I am going to lay down a small carrying bag that will help us move the body after we are complete, it will only take a moment and Roxy won't feel anything except a slight pinch."

"Okay." Ben sat for a moment, petting Roxy again as her attention moved back to him. He looked her in the eyes and saw everything that he had been through in the last ten years. He saw the many days and nights that Roxy kept watch in the various homes they lived in. From his parents' to the rental home to his grandmother's home, which he would eventually buy. She had been with Ben through two long-term relationships and those spaces in between. Those moments where Ben would lose his cool and get agitated at the mistakes Roxy would make, or just be angry at himself. Every time though, she would come right back to Ben, and loved Ben more than anyone else in the entire world. Ben in that moment felt so guilty because he knew that, while Roxy was only one piece of his world, to Roxy, Ben was her whole world.

It hurt Ben because this would be the last look that they would share. He looked over to the technician.

"It's time."

"Okay I'll just need her to lay down here where the bag is."

Ben stood up and Roxy did as well, with a few last limps, Ben asked Roxy to lay down. She did so instantly and obediently, just as she had done many times before without hesitation. As she lay down on her side, Ben just looked down at her sweet face. She was panting from the day that was to only get hotter, and Ben stroked her flowing fur.

The technician pulled the needle out from a bag and prepared it. He cleaned off the leg where the injection was to go and gave Ben a look. Ben just gave a nod and with that, he looked back down at Roxy. He didn't watch the injection go in, but heard Roxy's leg quiver back as the needle went in.

With the injection, the panting started to slowly fade. Ben continued to pet the same spot, in near disbelief that it was all happening. The panting faded further and eventually turned to silence. Roxy's eyes did not close. They simply went blank and the life was gone. The vibrancy had faded and there were to be no more nights at Ben's bed side, no more barks at dogs walking by or jumping for joy when Ben would return from a shoot.

It was gone and Ben slowly stood up. He had to assist the technician to carry the body out to the car where she was to be cremated. The body was easily placed in the car and the trunk was closed.

Ben thanked the technician and watched the car pull away.

As he walked back into the house, the first thing Ben noticed was the quiet air now present. The first thing he did was walk over to Roxy's bed and lay on it. As he did, the tears poured out for what felt like an eternity. The crying went on and on, but Roxy was not there to nudge Ben, to remind Ben that it was all going to be okay.

The cries were for Roxy not being there, the devastating loss of another companion in Ben's life. He had seen too much death in such a short amount of time of living.

The other part that Ben had to deal with deep down was whether or not he made the right decision. If money wasn't an issue, could he have done more to keep Roxy healthy, could he have made more appointments? Was all of this enough or did he make this decision for his own financial reasons?

It was a guilt that Ben was never truly ever to get over and even now bothers Ben deep down.

Blue Valentine

The expectation was high for Ben not to ruin the senior prom for Lily the same way he had her junior prom. It actually wasn't even an expectation as much as it was a demand. She had told him from the start that he didn't even have to go if he wasn't going to have fun with her. Of course, Ben insisted it would be different.

It was something about Lily being the center of attention, or at least the attention being pulled away from Ben that bothered him. He just didn't enjoy not being the one that everyone might be looking at or wanting to talk to. Maybe a touch of jealousy, maybe some sort of narcissism; either way it was a way that would create a complete shut down when left unchecked.

As Lily was getting ready at her grandparent's home, Ben laid around on her bed watching from afar. They listened to music and talked about life. Everything felt nice and Ben felt fine.

The first tearing down of his calm demeanor was the lipstick that Lily would eventually don for the night. He hated when Lily wore lipstick, in fact, he hated lipstick in general. Something about the glimmery red texture up close always made him physically sick. He had asked her not to wear it, but she wanted to feel pretty and this helped her in that goal. It was the first small defeat for Ben that would begin the breaking down of his ability to stay positive.

As Lily's friends started to gather the attention was further pulled onto the fact that this was her senior prom. Her night to shine and have fun. Ben had his suit on, but none of his friends would be there, his family was not there to take any pictures, there was no support structure for him. He felt isolated and as a result, began to internalize all of his emotions.

When the pictures started, he outright refused to smile and this was something that did not go unnoticed. Time and time again, Lily's family and her friends' families would exclaim aloud to smile everyone, or shout directly to Ben to smile at all. Even Lily whispered under her breath to him to just fake it for the cameras. She could read what was happening and knew that something might be up.

"Don't ruin tonight for me, you promised me you wouldn't."

"I'm sorry, I just don't feel good, my stomach I think, I'll be fine in a little bit."

"Ok, but you still don't have to come even now, I would understand."

Ben should have walked away at that moment, but he always had this way of lying so well that he would make it all make sense even for himself. It was like he was not only convincing Lily but also himself. Before that statement he didn't have any stomach pain, but maybe now all of a sudden, he did, that was surely the culprit.

As the group left, they were treated to a limo ride over to the venue for the dance. It was cheesy but again everyone soaked it in except Ben. Maybe if he knew at the time that it would be the last limo ride he would take outside of filming someone's wedding or event, he would have appreciated it more. Instead, he sat in his seat with a flat affect on his face, not caving to singing along with everyone else enjoying the music or the few hours of fun destined for the night.

Lily sat across from Ben and gave him a look that he would never forget. It was one that was filled with youthful glee that was drained so quickly when she looked at him. At the same time though, it was as if she was trying to nudge him across a bridge that would lead to letting go, taking away the grip of cynicism and just enjoying life. Despite the many opportunities that night would present for Lily to reach her arm out to try to pull Ben over that bridge, he wouldn't take a single one. Instead, he held firm in the idea that this whole night was frivolous.

As they entered the venue, the class of 2010 was trickling in. The music was already pumping and, despite being slowed down by the registration booth, Lily immediately wanted to get out to the dance floor.

Once they were set, she and her friends ran out. The dates for the friends followed quickly behind. For the first twenty minutes or so Ben had the excuse of wanting to find their assigned table. He took the time to do so and set his suit jacked on the back of a chair. There he sat, watching from way back in the room at the small crowd on the dancefloor. After a few songs, a slow interlude had come on. Lily rushed back to find Ben and asked him to come out to the floor with her. He did, and they had a nice slow dance together.

As soon as the partying started back up though, Ben wanted to leave. Lily tried her best to entice Ben. She came on to him, rubbed herself on him, and even promised some fun sex that night. Nothing seemed to convince him to want to stay though. After a little while, he returned back to the table which now had one of Lily's friends and their date.

He tried to talk to them about how silly the night was, and how little everyone knew about the world they were getting into was going to be. As if his two years in college somehow made him an expert on life.

"It's fun now, but just wait until they get into college, it is completely different. They don't even know."

"Yeah, but the least they can do is have fun tonight, right?"

"Sure, sure."

The couple left to go back to the dance floor. The attempt to bring others over to his side were of no use. The only one left being miserable was Ben, but now instead of being pulled to a side of joy by Lily, he was pulling her to a side of despair. After about an hour and a half of hardly interacting with anyone, Ben was ready to go home. He asked Lily if she wanted to go, which she instantly refused.

Ben was frustrated and started thinking to himself ways to convince her to leave with him. So, at first it was back to the stomach, then it was that it was getting late, any possible reason to go that he could come up with.

The only time he would get on the dance floor was now to argue with Lily, a gesture that was quickly picked up on by the teachers from the school. Teachers that Ben felt were at one time on his side, but were now addressing him like a villain.

"If all you're going to do is argue with Lily, then you need to leave right now." One teacher said to Ben from behind as he was sitting in his chair.

"She is trying to have a good time tonight, and all you're doing is ruining it." Another teacher said as he was trying to make his way to the dance floor.

Ben heard the messages loud and clear. He was not welcome and the entire venue was out to get him. So, he walked outside of the building and called his mother to come pick him up.

While he was waiting outside for her to come pick him up, Ben looked back at the room one more time. Now that he was committed to leaving, there was this biting inside him. All he had to do was just bite his lip, swallow his pride and just have fun. All Lily wanted was a good last prom with him, a fun night, and he was ruining it all.

He walked back through the doors, was making the way into the room when he was stopped by one of those same teachers again.

"Ben, you made your decision, let her have fun with her friends and go home, okay."

This was to be that moment of glory after a long night of not being able to just let go. Ben was going to ride back into the room like some sort of knight parading on horseback, returning from a victorious battle.

He could simply message his mother to go back home and the last hour of the dance could be pure ecstasy. With that simple statement though, the switch turned right back from happy to isolation. It was self-created isolation, but it was still the recipe that kept Ben from just having a good time.

As he turned around to walk back outside, his mother pulled up in the family minivan. He stepped in the car and put on a big explanation of how he was a victim. His mother saw right through it though, and tried to at least get Ben to see things from Lily's side of the fence. Ben knew he messed up, and knew he was in the wrong but that pride, that dark pride refused to let him see anything else.

It was a pride that would linger for a long time to come. Maybe if Ben had been able to turn it off faster that night, or even just made it to the point where he could have had fun with Lily, that stubborn standing in life would have melted away. Maybe the many years of fighting and tumult would have dissipated. It was one of those great 'what if' moments that Ben would look back on and wonder about.

He always saw Lily as lower than he was, not only because of his being older in age but just his attitude with life. However, it was probably Lily who always had it right from the beginning, but neither wanted to learn from the other to find some kind of common ground.

Dogtooth

The text message from Hector simply read "Here," and Ben was rushing down from the attic bedroom in his parents' home to the front yard. Out front was that white Infiniti Ben had sat shotgun in so many times before. The sun had just come up, and the adventure was just beginning.

Like something out of a mid-2000s bucket list, Hector, Ben, and their two work friends Joe and Paulwinder all were making the trek up to White Castle today. Yes, completely inspired by the movie, this was the day that all four young men were deciding to carpool up to try the slider burgers as a collective unit.

After Ben got in, the next house was Joe's, who Ben and Hector first met through the after-school job of cleaning dishes at a nearby retirement community. Joe was one of the first people who introduced himself to the reserved Ben, and when Hector started there, he introduced the two. Everyone quickly became friends and this was the first time that they were doing something outside of normal work shifts.

Joe slowly made his way to the car, seeming a little groggier due to the early morning start. He mentioned he would probably be taking a nap during the drive.

Paulwinder almost didn't even make it with the group, as when they arrived at his house, they didn't receive a text back or an answer when they started calling. Jumping from Joe to Ben to Hector, they all started reaching out and by some sheer amount of luck he just appeared from the front door, right as they were about to leave. The reasoning behind everything was his phone dying and not realizing the early leaving time. He made it though, and the four of them were off to New Jersey.

Ben was armed with the digital camcorder his parents had bought a few months prior to document the trip. Compared to future road trips, this one would rank very low but at the time it felt like a big one.

Once they were on the New Jersey Turnpike, the early morning energy started to subside. Paul and Joe were asleep in the backseat and Ben could feel his eyes getting heavy. The only thing keeping him awake was Hector's insistence that he stay up for support, giving Ben a nice arm punch whenever he noticed him drifting off.

"Stay awake."

"Why?"

"So I don't crash." Hector would comment, as if that would actually happen.

Before making it up to White Castle, Hector decided to make a pit stop in Philadelphia so they could check out the famous cheesesteaks. As they drove in the city, the only thing Ben kept thinking about was how overwhelming all the traffic and bustle was. He was glad Hector was driving, because it would have been simply too difficult for him to navigate through.

As they drove around trying to find a parking spot, Hector swore he saw the dance group the Jabbawockeez, which Ben filmed as quick as he could get the camera rolling. This was something that, even with the footage, is hard to make out, but down the road the video would get a few thousand views on YouTube.

They finally found a place to park and they were off to have their first culinary adventure of the day. At this one corner in Philly there stood two separate cheesesteak food stands which different people would argue on who tasted better. All of the friends ordered from both places and while Hector and Joe would eat now, Ben and Paul were saving their full appetites for White Castle.

Ben was hoping that either later that day or tomorrow he could sit down with Lily and they could try some of the food together.

After walking around the city for a little bit longer, the road trip was back in full swing. Now with everyone properly refreshed and having the legs stretched, the final forty-five minutes of the journey passed in no time at all.

As they got off the highway, the excitement was mounting for everyone. They saw the sign for White Castle as they hit their exit and knew it was only a few minutes away. Chanting aloud "White Castle," the small group could not wait to just simply see the building itself. Once they could see it, they were cheering and Hector was honking the horn.

Pulling into the parking lot, Ben could feel his mouth watering. He had eaten nothing to this point so he could fully take in every delicious bite.

It was now right around noon, the lunch rush was in full swing, and these four young men were going to make the jobs for every employee at this fast-food haven that much harder. Each one of them was going to order the Crave Case, which was a self-contained cardboard box filled with fifty sliders each. They all wanted to see how many they could eat and then save plenty for their friends/family back home.

After a half hour of waiting, the orders were up and each of them sat at one table inside. They opened their cases and grabbed a slider. Before taking a bite, Hector made a small speech.

"We made it guys, we're here and about to dig into some amazing burgers. Are you all ready?"

The group cheered and they all bounced the burgers together in the air before everyone took their own bite. It was an explosion of flavor that for Ben was everything he had ever hoped for. He loved it and was so happy that were all able to make this trip happen.

As the meal went on, slowly each member of the group couldn't eat anymore. First was Joe, who complained even before eating a slider that he felt that cheesesteak didn't sit right with him, then Paul, who wanted to save more for his family; Hector, and finally Ben, who managed to get twelve burgers down with fries before finally having to give up.

While the group was reflecting on the meal, Joe had stepped outside to lay down on the small patch of grass with his case. It was a cool day, so he fell asleep again and only woke up when the others wrapped up inside.

Everyone else sat on the grass around Joe and kept reflecting on how they made it and that they all needed to go on more adventures in the future together.

Hector suggested that they take a picture in front of the building. Ben rushed to his car to get the camera and get everything set up in the photo mode. As he did, Joe finally got up from the grass, noticing all the ants that had made their way into his crave case. He barely made it through three sliders and the ants claimed the rest.

The others offered to give him sliders from their own collections, but Joe denied the offer. He changed the subject to getting the picture done and together they all put their arms around one another.

A few exposures later, they were all headed back to Hector's car. They waved their goodbyes to the restaurant and headed back home. The journey back was again filled with naps and small talk about school, work and life. It was the kind of car ride that only happens once in a blue moon. No incidents or confrontations, just peace with four young guys living out an adventure from a movie they all enjoyed.

Megan

It was pretty early in the morning when Ben picked me up. It was also our first-time meeting and I was going with him while he was filming a wedding. I guess it was out of some kind of curiosity to see what it was like to film a wedding, so I was the one who suggested it in the first place. Although looking back now, it was a pretty dumb decision to do that for our first date.

It might have been October, but I remember it being an unusually hot day for that month. I'm pretty sure it either got up to or felt like 100 degrees, no exaggerations at all. Everyone was sweating and I felt so bad for the bride in her heavy dress, dealing with that. It was mainly outdoors too.

At one point Ben was getting flustered because his cameras were overheating. It was kind of cute watching him get worked up and sweating through his shirt. He was trying to play it somewhat cool with me but I could tell he was mad.

Something told me from the very start of that day that this wasn't really going to work out and turn into anything long term. So, I started taking stock of all the guests to see if maybe I could flirt with one of them. No one caught my eye, though, so I just hung out, pretending to be Ben's "assistant" for the day. Not that anyone ever questioned it, but I still had to be prepared for people occasionally coming up to me and asking questions about the cameras or that kind of stuff.

I was a research assistant, I didn't know the first thing, but I could pretend like I did. It was fun getting the chance to pretend for the day, especially since I wasn't having any good chemistry with Ben that day. He didn't even try to hold my hand or give me a kiss at any point.

When they served dinner at the restaurant they booked, I left for a little bit to another small diner across the street. That feeling persisted of not taking any stock in Ben and so I started chatting with my server, who was a decent enough looking guy. I told him about my day and we exchanged numbers. A week later we would go on a much better date than the one I had with Ben.

I still had to see things through, though, with this wedding. After passing the time I walked back over the restaurant where things were starting to wind down. Ben looked tired and his shirt was barely tucked in anymore. The sweat stains were thick and the fatigue was obvious.

Ben gave the option of just dropping me back off home if I wanted to, which I thought was courteous enough, but honestly, I just wanted to get laid at that point. When we got back to Ben's place, I offered to shower with him but instead Ben wanted us to take turns.

I showered first and then he showered after me. The sex was pretty good, I got off, but it wasn't anything memorable.

The next morning Ben offered to make or get me breakfast. I could tell that he didn't really want to though and so I said I was okay, when I was really starving, and he drove me back home.

There wasn't much conversation to speak of that drive back. Just music playing loud enough so that the silence wasn't deafening. Then after that I didn't really hear much more from Ben, until maybe a month or two later.

"Hey, sorry I haven't been in touch. Just dealing with a crazy schedule here."

"That's okay, I kind of figured you might ghost me so that night of the wedding I actually gave my number to the server across the street from the restaurant. He isn't a keeper either, but we had a nice time and he still talks to me."

"I'm glad you had a good time with someone you met that night."

"Thanks, all the best to you."

"All the best to you, too."

After that message I never did hear from Ben again. I kind of didn't want to, I liked him enough to spend an entire day on something that wasn't even really a date. I went back to his place and that was it. He is someone that you want to forget, but for some odd reason that memory always remained so vivid in my mind. So strange yet so mundane all at once.

Gone Girl

After a few weeks of planning, the day for filming had finally arrived. Ben had the storyline all set and the style was an action/martial arts music video. The band was on board and Ben even managed to find a local stunt studio to help with the choreography for the day. All the pieces were lined up and the perfect location, a loft in the heart of Baltimore, was rented out.

Ben's two closest film friends, Nick and Everett were going to be overseeing all the technical aspects of the shoot. From the lighting to the camera work, these two brought the skills of what normally would take five or six. Ben only called them in for his biggest productions. It was an exciting change of pace and a production that would help solidify everyone with what they were trying to do in their own careers.

The three had never worked on any kind of action-style video before, so it was fresh, uncharted territory.

The members of the band slowly began to arrive and the excitement was building. As the members of the stunt group made their way in, the stage was set for what was going to be a long day, but one that would produce a final product for all to be happy with.

Nick and Everett were setting the lights in the hallway space for the first scene as Ben went over with everyone what they were going to be doing on the day. The overall story was one of vengeance, a man trying to find his kidnapped girlfriend. A cliché martial arts story, but that was always the point, a theme only aided by the fact that Ben had recently split up with Lily. It was his first shoot since then and he was eager to try and impress her, whether he realized it or not.

The main people were brought into the hallway after Nick and Everett were ready and they began doing some light run-through set ups before even rolling any cameras. The goal for the shot was to hide a long take by using strong blocking to their advantage. This broke down to basically positioning the camera around kicks, punches, blocks, etc. to make it look like they weren't editing but was actually heavily edited.

It was working; not just good, but really good. The shots were looking amazing and the action choreography was great. The big selling point was the use of fake weapons, which on camera looked amazing, despite being rubber imitations of the real thing. It was an amazing day so far.

It started to turn though, when one of the lead members of the stunt group began to question the way in which the video was being filmed. Whether from his own experiences with making videos, or his inability to see the vision that Ben and the team had, he first brought something to Ben.

"Are you sure this is how you want to film the project?"

"How do you mean?"

"Like it seems like you are going to be missing a lot of what we are doing on camera, like a lot of cuts and such. Just doesn't seem the right way to do it. Just putting it out there."

Ben had shrugged this off as nothing more than a little bit of questioning. He went on to explain the style they were going for and thought nothing more of it.

After getting all the shots wrapped, it was time for a quick break as the team went on to find the next area to film at. During this break in the action though, that very same person went over to talk with the band members; however, instead of questioning what Ben and the team were doing, he explained to them how everything was wrong. He showed them his own videos and went into great detail about how it should be done. He had overstepped his place in the shoot.

The leader of the band then pulled Ben aside just as they were about to get into their second set up and asked what was going on. Now that the thought had been placed in his mind, he felt that maybe there was something wrong going on with the video. Of course, now Ben had to play defense, as not only did he have to explain why this method was okay, but also tip toe around simply calling the stunt member an idiot. If he did that, he would risk losing all the stunt members since he was one of the co-founders of the group.

It was a tough situation and even worse, Nick and Everett began to question their own way of filming as well. Instead of sticking to their methods, they compromised for the next set up just a few minutes before filming was set to go. Rather than having a lot of edits to coincide with the action, they filmed things wider and with more of a long-take mentality. It quickly became clear that this wasn't working. The choreography looked stiff, less convincing, and it just plain didn't look good.

Even still, the drama of the day continued as the stunt member was now simply trying to leave the shoot altogether. He was arguing with the other founding member when Ben happened to walk in to grab a water bottle from the prepping room. Ben was already irate from him undermining the vision and words were exchanged.

As the confrontation grew louder, more members from all sides came into the room. It was clear that things weren't working and the tension was too great. Inevitably the day was considered a wash and the amount of footage captured would really only account for about twenty percent of what they needed to make the music video happen.

They had to pack everything up and Ben would end up breaking even on all the money that was spent on wardrobe, rental space and props.

After they got everything packed up, Ben, Nick and Everett all decided to grab dinner at a burger place that wasn't too far. Ben was still venting over his break-up and lamenting over the failed shoot. Nick and Everett did their parts, trying to keep everything positive. They joked, talked, and enjoyed some good food. Despite the lost day, things had felt somewhat alright by the end of it.

After dinner, the three went their separate ways. Ben went home to Roxy, who was excited as ever to greet him at the door. Ben sat down in front of the couch for a little while and on his phone, he still had messages to go through from Lily, as the two were still communicating over Instagram. Between that, watching a random TV show; and playing on a random dating app on his phone, Ben killed the rest of the evening.

It was a routine that was all too familiar to Ben, and one that would go on for months, years to come. His constant messaging of Lily, trying to somehow win her back was a sad motif, that was only egged on by every passing response she would give. Any hint that she might come back was all Ben needed, yet at the same time, he would continue to try to date and meet new women constantly. It was again a source of needed attention.

The music video would never be made. Despite trying to schedule another day of filming, and finding other resources, the band grew impatient. It was a project that, if it had happened the way everyone wanted it to, probably would have been amazing. The pieces were all there and if it weren't for the ego-fueled drama from those involved, maybe even a little bit of that vision would have happened.

As it all played out though, it wasn't meant to be and it was yet another reason for Ben to move further into the world of events and weddings, where he was finding himself more and more. It was one of those fateful days that changes a person, making them want to branch out less, even if that place they wanted to go was creatively driven.

Ben would fall asleep with the phone close to him, as Lily mentioned that their love was like the film *The Notebook*, a strong comparison to a film Ben had yet to watch. He knew what he was going to be doing tomorrow.

The Glass House

Going to see Tony after school and watch TRL was an amazing privilege for Ben, one that made him rush through his homework duties at his grandmother's before being picked up by his father after work. It was a short window of time and not something he could experience every day.

Today was a day that afforded Ben the time to go do that, but it came with a caveat from his grandmother. She had mentioned that Tony hadn't been feeling well the past few days. Something that Ben had, by this age, known about and even seen with Tony having to go to the hospital but never given much thought to. Tony might have cystic fibrosis, but he was fine otherwise, Ben would think to himself.

As he ran out the door to Tony's house, well, Tony's mother's home, Ben's aunt, Ben began to think about this warning more. It seemed ominous to Ben, like he needed to act differently. Was this his grandmother's way of saying don't be too hyperactive today, don't ask a lot of questions, don't try to do too much? It all seemed so strange, as this line of thinking never really struck Ben before. It was just odd.

The first change Ben felt was, instead of just bursting through the door to sit at the couch next to Tony, he knocked at the door. There was a hesitation, maybe brought on by the clear coughing he could hear from Tony before he made it all the way up the steps. As he knocked a few taps, Tony yelled for him to come in.

In a bit more of a raspy tone, Tony said 'hey' to Ben as he was watching the top music videos of the day on MTV. The countdown would normally have meant an automatic spot on the couch next to Tony, but today Ben only felt as if he could make it a few steps into the room. He felt reserved, shy, quiet, all of these things that would become a staple of Ben later in life made their way out right here and now.

Ben divided his time looking at the screen and then watching Tony, who was working on some school work. It was awkward; and weird. Ben knew he needed to say something, but what should he say? He didn't want to even ask how Tony was feeling because the constant coughing made it obvious that he wasn't. The music videos playing were nothing new or exciting for Ben to comment on, school wasn't close to being over for the summer break. It just felt blank. All of it felt wrong.

After a few minutes of nothing, Ben simply said "see ya" to Tony and was out of the house. He felt so stupid, and as he ran back down to his grandmother's house, he shed a few tears. He was so angry at himself and instantly regretted not saying anything at all to Tony, but it felt wrong, all of it. Something just in the air was off.

The next day, Ben didn't even have a chance to go down to the house because of the amount of school work he had to get through. The day after that, Tony was being rushed off to the hospital. For the next few months, Tony would stay in a coma, one from which he would never emerge.

Early on in the hospital visits, Ben's grandmother would ask him what had happened during his silent visit. She mentioned that Tony asked her about it the day before he went into his coma. Ben had no answer for his awkward actions, but knew it was a result of those few words his grandmother spoke that day.

Maybe if she had said nothing, Ben would have treated Tony normally, they would have sat and watched TV one last time together before things would change. One last sweet memory before he passed away, but rather, what was left was just this strange awkward moment before he was trapped in his own dream state for months on end until the plug was finally pulled.

Ben never let himself forget that and hoped that, at some point, maybe Tony forgot about that one day and remembered all the other great moments they had together. One could hope that maybe this was true.

Children of Men

As Ben walked through the bookstore, he was hoping to find some interesting manga to read for that upcoming weekend. Japanese manga was that perfect crossroad between reading and watching an anime. At the time there were only a few Japanese shows on the air, so looking through the manga area of any bookstore could yield an interesting find. Today he was taking the risk on a series called *Black Cat*, which was a few volumes deep and had a nice art style.

Ben, who was still working his way through his learner's permit, had to drive with an adult present who on this day was an old family friend. After this short trip, the next stop was Ben's cousin's birthday party but the timing was still early. So, at the suggestion of the friend, they drove back to his house, an innocent enough gesture.

As they drove back from the store, the conversation on Ben's mind was the one that he shared with this friend several times, which of course was about girls. Ben had yet to be in a relationship, or to really have more than a passing time with girls. He was a bit on the heavier side and always felt self-conscious about his body and himself. He always had this feeling that maybe things just wouldn't work out and he would be lonely for a long time.

All these things were, of course, disputed by the friend, he said that Ben was a handsome guy, he would find someone, it was just a matter of time. Ben never took this as meaning much though, since of course an old friend would say that. He would rather be hearing that from a girl he liked.

As the conversation went on, there was a sexual element brought into the fold. Ben, being a blossoming teenager, was curious about sex, not having had sex at this point in his life. It was a topic which this family friend was never shy about chatting to Ben with either. Unlike Ben's parents who would never want to discuss such things, this was really the only outlet for Ben to get thoughts out too.

They talked about how it must feel and again, this friend assured Ben that, in due time, he would have plenty of experience with the opposite sex. Don't rush it, he would mention, live life and when the time comes it will come.

Even at the slightest talk of sex or thinking of it at this age for Ben made his libido go up and just through talking about it, Ben felt a certain rush come over his body. He felt like he wanted to masturbate, but with today being a day away from home there wouldn't really be an opportunity to do so.

As they pulled into the driveway of the friend's home, the topic of sex continued on. Sometimes the topic would be reintroduced by Ben, other times the friend. The only constant was the drinking that the family friend was doing throughout.

Alcohol was much like sex to Ben, a strange part of adulthood that he would have to wait on. Ben truly wanted to wait until he was twenty-one to begin drinking, even if he had at one point tried a sip of Southern Comfort in his parents' cabinet when they were asleep. He thought it tasted disgusting and felt that if this is what alcohol tasted like all the time, there was certainly no rush to start drinking. Experiences like that and the fact that his parents never carried alcohol themselves kept Ben from ever really drinking when he was underage.

This friend, though, was quite liberal when it came to alcohol, even offering some to Ben, who politely declined. As he continued to drink more, Ben was feeling a bit tired, as they had started rather early in the day for a Saturday. Between that and a long week at school, a certain amount of fatigue was setting in.

Ben wanted to relax and the family friend offered a massage. This was nothing new or out of the ordinary, Ben had received many massages over the years from this friend. Whether that be on the back, the feet, or the head. He was always good at them, and they always seemed to help so Ben said it was okay.

After a few motions of the hands over the shoulders, the first ask was to lift the shirt off, a fine piece to help with any kind of muscle relief. Ben thought nothing of it, so he quickly took the shirt off.

The friend moved his hands up and down the back a few times, making sure to work out the muscles, kicking out any kinks. From there, he moved down to the feet, pulling Ben's socks off, again a harmless act. He rubbed each toe and moved up and down each foot. The transition then became the legs, each of which he took special time with. Moving further up and down each one.

As it happened, there was a certain sensation that Ben had begun to feel as the friend moved up his legs. It was a tingling type of feeling that he had never really experienced before and a strange rush. The friend eased over the area a few times but seemed to be focusing his attention more as Ben let out a twitch each time he did so.

For Ben everything was starting to get mixed up, he knew his attraction was strictly to girls, yet here he was getting some bit of a turn on from this older guy rubbing on his leg. He didn't know what to make of it. Then came the inevitable question.

"Do you want to take your pants off?"

"Should I? I don't know."

"I'm not going to force you or anything, it's up to you."

With that said, Ben slowly made his way to his pants button and undid them. That was all he did, he stopped short of actually pulling them off, he needed another moment. As he did though the hands of the friend started to massage right at the top of the hips, providing ever more strange sensations to Ben. In the same maneuver he took hold of each side of the pants and pulled them the rest of the way from Ben's body. He was down to only his underwear and the rubbing continued on.

After the touches worked their way further up the leg, the sensation was undeniable to Ben. It was as if this person knew exactly where to touch to cause every stimulation to work their way up and down Ben's entire body. Ben was fully erect and was trying to play it cool for the time being.

"Flip over."

"What?"

"Flip over and I can get the front next."

Ben slowly flipped his body over and there was no hiding the erection now. As soon as he did, the friend took notice. He saw it etched out in the boxers and took another drink of his wine in a kind of toast to the visage of it.

All of it should have stopped there, but Ben was excited, confused and overwhelmed with so many different emotions. He had no time to process it all, really, and through all of these raging hormones, he slid the boxers off, revealing his full naked body to the friend. He immediately took his hand and, -in a gliding motion, rubbed it up and down Ben's frame.

He took the time to admire Ben's penis and, after a few passing motions, to get Ben even more aroused he asked if he could suck on it. Ben froze up, again within a matter of thirty minutes he had gone from a tired teenage boy to being completely naked in the home of an old trusted friend. He was not attracted to the friend at all, but merely aroused by the situation.

This whole time he was not picturing his hands touching him, but rather some girl he was fantasizing about at the time. This was one of only a few times that Ben felt himself carried outside of his body. He was looking down on himself picturing all of this with the girl of his dreams.

Through every one of these factors playing against him, Ben agreed to the gesture and the friend began performing fellatio on Ben until he finished. It felt amazing, a far cry from anything simple masturbation could bring about and again picturing some beautiful woman made everything feel all the better. Ben never looked down at the friend, never made eye contact, just closed his eyes and took this entirely new sensation in.

After they finished the friend brought in a box of tissues and Ben wiped himself off. The time for the birthday party was upon them and Ben got dressed as the friend finished off his wine.

At the birthday party Ben sat quietly, watching his young cousin, who was turning eight today, run around with his friends in the distance. It was a sweet portrait of sheer innocence that Ben had lost once as he watched Tony succumb to CF, but now further removed as his first sexual act was taken away by this old friend of his father's. This friend sat with Ben's aunts and uncles, joking and carrying on as if nothing had even happened.

Lamb

It was an hour and a half to the location. A mundane drive that felt rather calming, the easy ability to contain all the anxiety simmering up to the surface. It was another day for filming a wedding and Ben wanted nothing to do with it.

He felt ever more removed today as his uncle was visiting from South Carolina, bringing up the remainder of his grandmother's belongings, who just recently passed away. He wanted more time to talk with him, but had to leave if he was to make to the location on time.

The car was brand new, but had rust spots all over it. They weren't visible to the naked eye, but Ben knew all too well that his pride and joy was forever tarnished. Not even the manufacturer would claim responsibility for the defect, it was bird droppings caked on according to their "experts," in the matter. Less than 10,000 miles, Ben would think to himself each time he looked at it.

The gear was not Ben's but rather belonged to the owner of the studio that contracted Ben for the job. It was only two bags and two tripods. All the audio, cameras and lenses were efficiently packed away. Always a good feeling not having to use his own equipment. Less chance of something breaking that he would have to pay for later on.

When he walked in the building there was no one around, but voices could be heard in a nearby room. The place was an old cigar packing facility, long abandoned and refinished to service an entire wedding day.

This special occasion marked the third time Ben was filming for this particular family. Something that actually felt pretty special for him, like he obviously was doing a pretty good job to be the first person a family thought of three times over to cover their children's wedding days. It was this mild familiarity that provided a bit of ease as Ben worked the nerves up to walk into the bridal room.

That initial awkwardness, though, was always unavoidable, especially when walking into a room filled with women in thin robes. He could always just tell they were tensing up, pulling the sash's tighter, and reading to see if he might say something creepy or off putting.

Instead, Ben would ring out the same turn of phrase he always did to put people at ease. "The best thing you can do for me all day is pretend I'm not here."

They would laugh or at least chuckle and then, just like that, Ben was a ghost again. Just sitting back in the shadows, seeming inconspicuous as possible. It worked well today and the social interactions were minimal from the family.

It was a cold and windy day, but the photographers still insisted on taking the couple outside for photos. Sure, it was pretty with the brick industrial backdrop for a majority of the photos, but the bride especially was not happy about it. Neither was Ben, who took any chance to walk back inside the building to warm up.

After some photos of the couple, they were allowed back inside, but only briefly as the bridal party photos were next. Now that the sun was starting to set and the wind was getting heavier the excuses for Ben to walk away became even greater. The process took even longer, as the couple insisted on having their dog in the photos. This was not a well-behaved dog either.

The couple was done with being outside, and the remainder of the night was spent indoors, until the sparkler send-off at the very end of the evening.

The Ketubah was to be signed next. Ben wanted to wear a traditional kippah, but the photographer yelled at him for it. He argued that since Ben wasn't Jewish it was in poor taste to wear it. Ben just enjoyed the feeling of comradery in the moment, but after a slight back and forth he took it off. No joy it seems on this occasion.

That dog was in the ceremony as well, barking and in general being a bit of a distraction from the couple. It was an abbreviated Jewish ceremony, and within 30 minutes they were officially married, well ceremonially married, as the Ketubah signing had been the real marriage moment.

The rest of the night was filled with toasts, dancing and the usual drunken stupidity that came with most weddings Ben had filmed to this point. Make sure to get grandma on the dance floor, and the cousins, and the parents (they are footing the bill after all).

Ben stress ate that night, as he almost always did during wedding nights. He had some panko crusted chicken with a pepper medley and macaroni with cheese. After that, he had two whole donuts from the donut display that was set up in the corner and another hour later, he had a slice of cake. He kept feeling hungry, so he just kept on eating.

The last song that evening would be *First Date* by Blink 182, a song that Ben almost learned to play when he took guitar lessons as a kid. It felt ironic to hear it tonight, doing something that completely kept him from any kind of creative pursuit he had yearning inside.

After getting everyone outside of the venue, they had their sparkler send off. A joyous, minute-long excursion which took far longer to get working than it did to actually complete.

That was it, yet it felt hollow. That was it, but there was no fanfare for Ben to enjoy. That was the last wedding that Ben would ever film, he was done, officially retired. Yet something about it just didn't feel real.

As he drove home, barely staying awake because it was so late, Ben did not feel a sense of any accomplishment whatsoever. Nine years of wedding videography with really nothing more than money to show for it. Nothing more than just things that were purchased with that same money. No accolades, awards, honors, or even a retirement party. Was anything there that should be celebrated?

The next day Ben had horrible diarrhea and had to drop the equipment back off to the studio owner in Baltimore. He worked up enough energy to do that, and then get back home where he slept for most of the day. His parents didn't mention or ask much about the shoot, they just talked about nothing while watching some home renovation show that was playing in the background on the small kitchen television.

Fargo

Ben never enjoyed sleeping on the weekends. In his mind, it only meant the weekend would go by faster before the school week would start again. Weekends were sacred and Ben needed to spend each one to their fullest. The first way to kick off any weekend proper was taking in all the new cartoon episodes that would air on Saturday mornings.

After that would come some time outside, followed by videogames, and maybe even a movie that the family had rented from Blockbuster the Friday night before. This Saturday in particular, though, would prove to be a special one.

On any ordinary Saturday, Ben's parents would always like to sleep in. Perhaps feeling burned out from a long work week or just wanting the extra time to relax, they enjoyed the rest. Ben never quite understood it, but he also didn't understand why he couldn't have Doritos for breakfast either (besides that time he chipped his tooth on one in the morning maybe).

For some strange reason though, today both of Ben's parents were up even before he was. Something about spring cleaning that had his mom up at 7 a.m. 8 a.m. was usually the time for Ben to jump up, as that would start the four-hour long block of shows all the way to noon.

Perhaps because his mother was up, Ben's father was up today, too, just as early. However, instead of the usual project he had lined up, there was not really much for Ben's father to do today. Instead, he sat in the living room with Ben and began watching cartoon with his son.

Ben didn't say much at first because he thought maybe his dad would spend just a few moments making sure Ben wasn't watching anything inappropriate and then leave again. This day though, he stayed and was actually asking Ben about the characters on the different series.

"So, what does the dog one do?"

"I told you dad, he's the main guy, and has to beat up all the bad guys."

"Oh, and so those are the bad guys right there?"

"Yeah, come on dad, aren't you watching?"

Ben's dad kept on asking questions like that all morning, learning the details of each show as Ben was getting excited more and more by the prospect of his dad learning all of it. It was like Ben was an encyclopedia, prepping his father for weeks of Saturday morning cartoon watching to come. Ben thought that if he taught his dad all the gaps, then he would have no reason not to watch the shows with him week to week.

Every minute of that morning felt special, and Ben's mother took the time to smile in on them as she was tidying up the house. She even snapped a photo or two with her handy 35mm camera that was sure to make an appearance at every family get together.

Who is to say whether that day was a genuine gesture that Ben's father felt like doing that particular Saturday, or if Ben's mother asked him to do it? Either way, that was one of the greatest Saturdays Ben had ever experienced in his life. It was at this perfect moment where the world held all the promise of a bright future, summer was soon approaching and all the attention a kid could crave was fulfilled.

For all the trials, mistakes, tribulations and hardship that would come upon Ben in the years following, this day was perfection. Even though a day like it would never happen again, Ben always wanted to tell his father thank you.

Afterword:

There is no perfection in being a parent like there is no perfection in being a son. I've done the best I can being one and I'll do the best I can until I'm done.

www.ingramcontent.com/pod-product-compliance
Lightning Source LLC
Chambersburg PA
CBHW051424290426
44109CB00016B/1422